This planner belongs to :

____

Twenty-three

January

S	M	T	W	T	F	S
1	2	3	4	5	6	7
8	9	10	11	12	13	14
15	16	17	18	19	20	21
22	23	24	25	26	27	28
29	30	31				

February

S	M	T	W	T	F	S
			1	2	3	4
5	6	7	8	9	10	11
12	13	14	15	16	17	18
19	20	21	22	23	24	25
26	27	28				

March

S	M	T	W	T	F	S
			1	2	3	4
5	6	7	8	9	10	11
12	13	14	15	16	17	18
19	20	21	22	23	24	25
26	27	28	29	30	31	

April

S	M	T	W	T	F	S
						1
2	3	4	5	6	7	8
9	10	11	12	13	14	15
16	17	18	19	20	21	22
23	24	25	26	27	28	29
30						

May

S	M	T	W	T	F	S
	1	2	3	4	5	6
7	8	9	10	11	12	13
14	15	16	17	18	19	20
21	22	23	24	25	26	27
28	29	30	31			

June

S	M	T	W	T	F	S
				1	2	3
4	5	6	7	8	9	10
11	12	13	14	15	16	17
18	19	20	21	22	23	24
25	26	27	28	29	30	

July

S	M	T	W	T	F	S
						1
2	3	4	5	6	7	8
9	10	11	12	13	14	15
16	17	18	19	20	21	22
23	24	25	26	27	28	29
30	31					

August

S	M	T	W	T	F	S
		1	2	3	4	5
6	7	8	9	10	11	12
13	14	15	16	17	18	19
20	21	22	23	24	25	26
27	28	29	30	31		

September

S	M	T	W	T	F	S
					1	2
3	4	5	6	7	8	9
10	11	12	13	14	15	16
17	18	19	20	21	22	23
24	25	26	27	28	29	30

October

S	M	T	W	T	F	S
1	2	3	4	5	6	7
8	9	10	11	12	13	14
15	16	17	18	19	20	21
22	23	24	25	26	27	28
29	30	31				

November

S	M	T	W	T	F	S
			1	2	3	4
5	6	7	8	9	10	11
12	13	14	15	16	17	18
19	20	21	22	23	24	25
26	27	28	29	30		

December

S	M	T	W	T	F	S
					1	2
3	4	5	6	7	8	9
10	11	12	13	14	15	16
17	18	19	20	21	22	23
24	25	26	27	28	29	30
31						

Year in Pixels

	J	F	M	A	M	J	J	A	S	O	N	D
1.												
2.												
3.												
4.												
5.												
6.												
7.												
8.												
9.												
10.												
11.												
12.												
13.												
14.												
15.												
16.												
17.												
18.												
19.												
20.												
21.												
22.												
23.												
24.												
25.												
26.												
27.												
28.												
29.												
30.												
31.												

Color Codes

Notes

January 2023

MONDAY	TUESDAY	WEDNESDAY	THURSDAY
2	3	4	5
9	10	11	12
16	17	18	19
23	24	25	26

January 2023

FRIDAY	SATURDAY	SUNDAY	NOTES
		1	○
			○
			○
			○
			○
6	7	8	○
			○
			○
			○
13	14	15	○
			○
			○
			○
20	21	22	○
			○
			○
			○
			○
27	28	29	30
			31

February 2023

MONDAY	TUESDAY	WEDNESDAY	THURSDAY
		1	2
6	7	8	9
13	14	15	16
20	21	22	23
27	28		

February 2023

FRIDAY	SATURDAY	SUNDAY	NOTES
3	4	5	○
			○
			○
			○
			○
10	11	12	○
			○
			○
			○
17	18	19	○
			○
			○
			○
24	25	26	○
			○
			○
			○
			○
			NOTES

March 2023

MONDAY	TUESDAY	WEDNESDAY	THURSDAY
		1	2
6	7	8	9
13	14	15	16
20	21	22	23
27	28	29	30

FRIDAY	SATURDAY	SUNDAY	NOTES
3	4	5	○
			○
			○
			○
10	11	12	○
			○
			○
			○
17	18	19	○
			○
			○
			○
24	25	26	○
			○
			○
			○
			○
31			NOTES

April 2023

MONDAY	TUESDAY	WEDNESDAY	THURSDAY
3	4	5	6
10	11	12	13
17	18	19	20
24	25	26	27

April 2023

FRIDAY	SATURDAY	SUNDAY	NOTES
	1	2	○
			○
			○
			○
			○
7	8	9	○
			○
			○
			○
14	15	16	○
			○
			○
			○
			○
21	22	23	○
			○
			○
			○
			○
28	29	30	NOTES

May 2023

MONDAY	TUESDAY	WEDNESDAY	THURSDAY
1	2	3	4
8	9	10	11
15	16	17	18
22	23	24	25
29	30	31	

May 2023

FRIDAY	SATURDAY	SUNDAY	NOTES
5	6	7	○
			○
			○
			○
			○
12	13	14	○
			○
			○
			○
19	20	21	○
			○
			○
			○
			○
26	27	28	○
			○
			○
			○
			○
			NOTES

June 2023

MONDAY	TUESDAY	WEDNESDAY	THURSDAY
			1
5	6	7	8
12	13	14	15
19	20	21	22
26	27	28	29

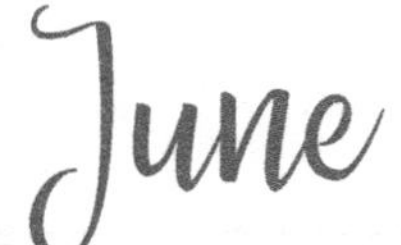

June

2023

FRIDAY	SATURDAY	SUNDAY	NOTES
2	3	4	○
			○
			○
			○
			○
9	10	11	○
			○
			○
			○
16	17	18	○
			○
			○
			○
			○
23	24	25	○
			○
			○
			○
			○
30			NOTES

July 2023

MONDAY	TUESDAY	WEDNESDAY	THURSDAY
3	4	5	6
10	11	12	13
17	18	19	20
24	25	26	27

July 2023

FRIDAY	SATURDAY	SUNDAY	NOTES
	1	2	○
			○
			○
			○
			○
7	8	9	○
			○
			○
			○
14	15	16	○
			○
			○
			○
			○
21	22	23	○
			○
			○
			○
			○
28	29	30	31

August 2023

MONDAY	TUESDAY	WEDNESDAY	THURSDAY
	1	2	3
7	8	9	10
14	15	16	17
21	22	23	24
28	29	30	31

August 2023

FRIDAY	SATURDAY	SUNDAY	NOTES
4	5	6	○
			○
			○
			○
			○
11	12	13	○
			○
			○
			○
18	19	20	○
			○
			○
			○
			○
25	26	27	NOTES

September 2023

MONDAY	TUESDAY	WEDNESDAY	THURSDAY
4	5	6	7
11	12	13	14
18	19	20	21
25	26	27	28

September 2023

FRIDAY	SATURDAY	SUNDAY	NOTES
1	2	3	○
			○
			○
			○
			○
8	9	10	○
			○
			○
			○
15	16	17	○
			○
			○
			○
			○
22	23	24	○
			○
			○
			○
			○
29	30		NOTES

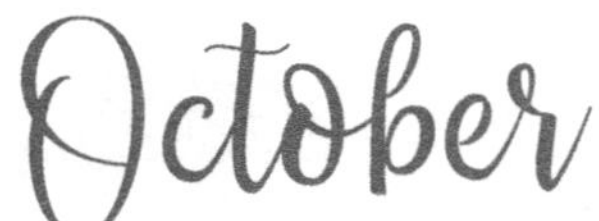

October 2023

MONDAY	TUESDAY	WEDNESDAY	THURSDAY
2	3	4	5
9	10	11	12
16	17	18	19
23	24	25	26

October 2023

FRIDAY	SATURDAY	SUNDAY	NOTES
		1	○
			○
			○
			○
			○
6	7	8	○
			○
			○
			○
13	14	15	○
			○
			○
			○
20	21	22	○
			○
			○
			○
			○
27	28	29	30
			31

November 2023

MONDAY	TUESDAY	WEDNESDAY	THURSDAY
		1	2
6	7	8	9
13	14	15	16
20	21	22	23
27	28	29	30

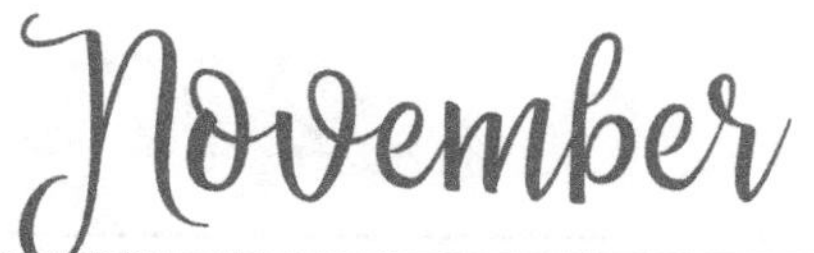

November 2023

FRIDAY	SATURDAY	SUNDAY	NOTES
3	4	5	○
			○
			○
			○
10	11	12	○
			○
			○
			○
17	18	19	○
			○
			○
			○
24	25	26	○
			○
			○
			○
			NOTES

December 2023

MONDAY	TUESDAY	WEDNESDAY	THURSDAY
4	5	6	7
11	12	13	14
18	19	20	21
25	26	27	28

December 2023

FRIDAY	SATURDAY	SUNDAY	NOTES
1	2	3	○
			○
			○
			○
			○
8	9	10	○
			○
			○
			○
15	16	17	○
			○
			○
			○
			○
22	23	24	○
			○
			○
			○
			○
29	30	31	NOTES

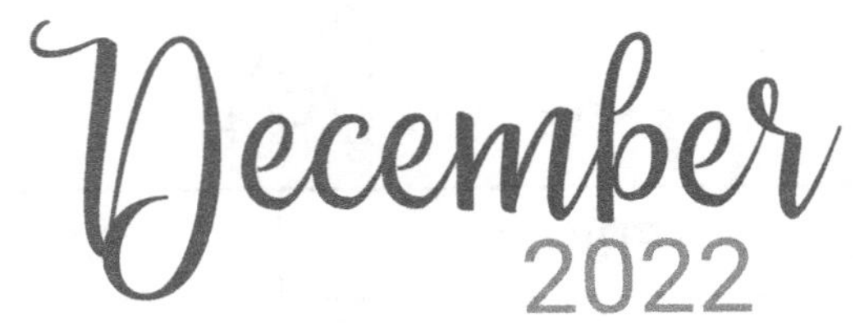

December
2022

01 THURSDAY

02 FRIDAY

03 SATURDAY

04 SUNDAY

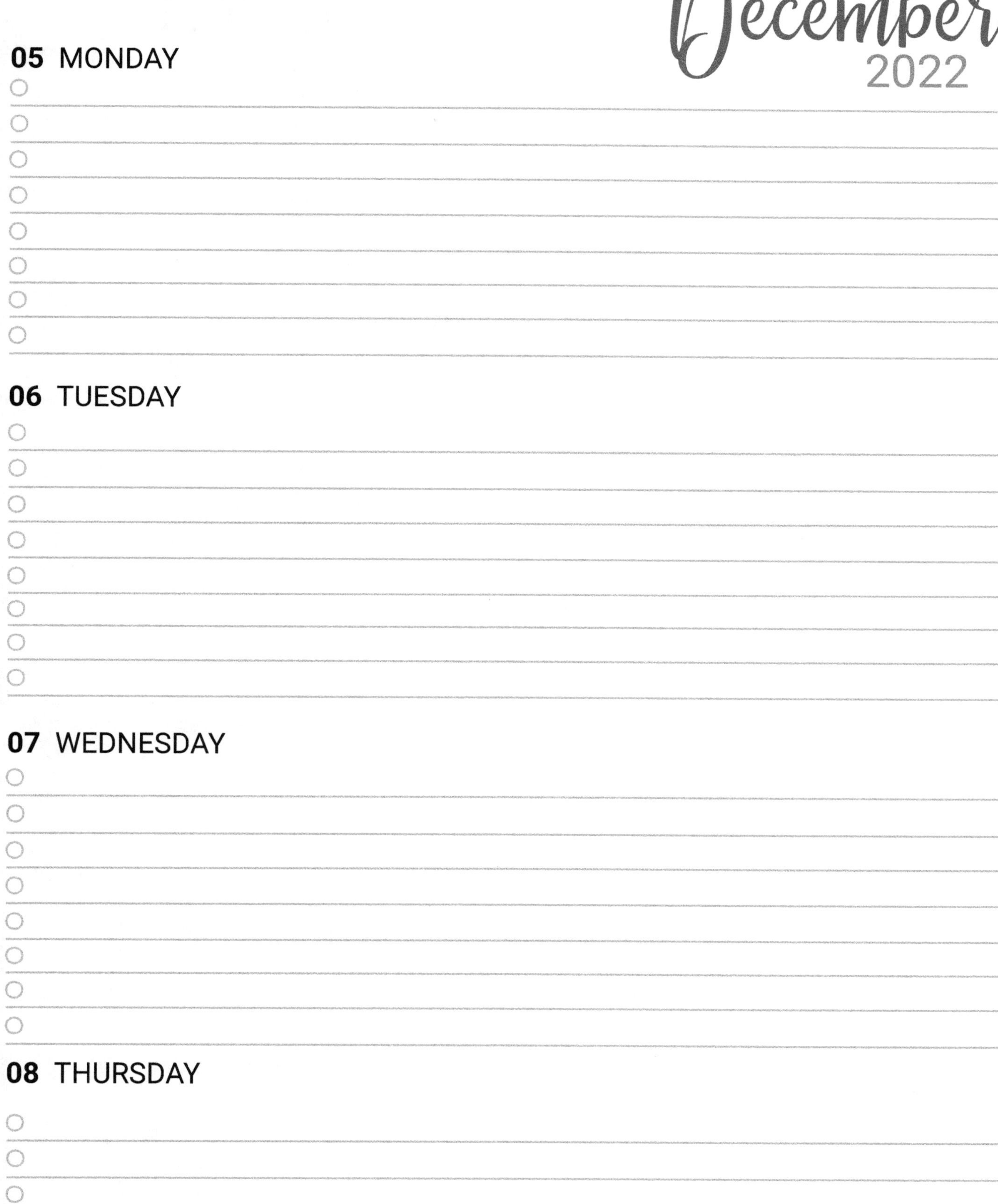

05 MONDAY

06 TUESDAY

07 WEDNESDAY

08 THURSDAY

December
2022

09 FRIDAY

10 SATURDAY

11 SUNDAY

12 MONDAY

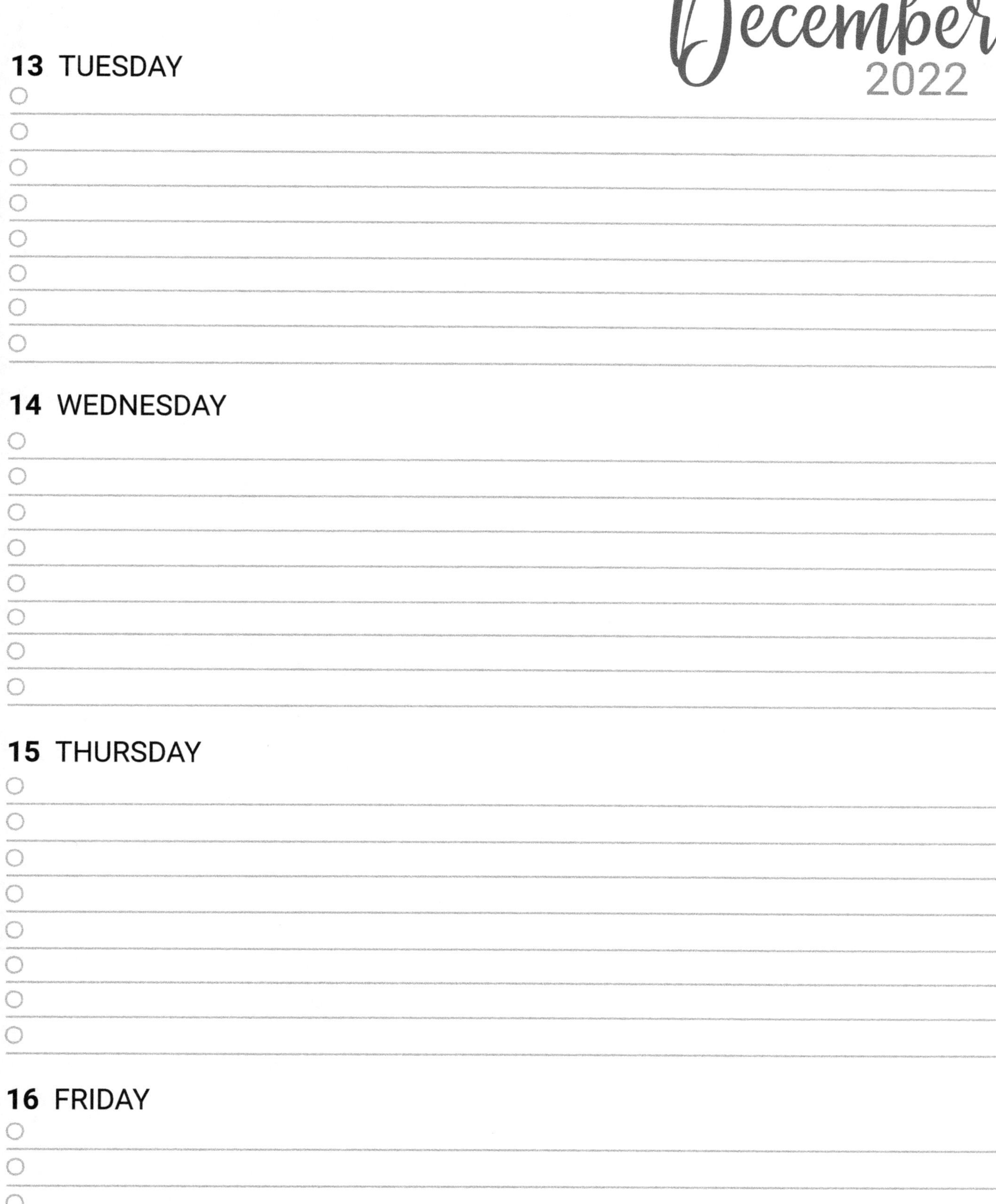

13 TUESDAY

14 WEDNESDAY

15 THURSDAY

16 FRIDAY

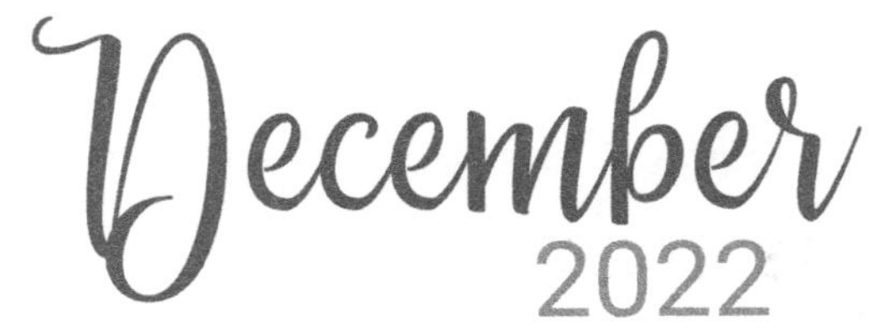

December
2022

17 SATURDAY

18 SUNDAY

19 MONDAY

20 TUESDAY

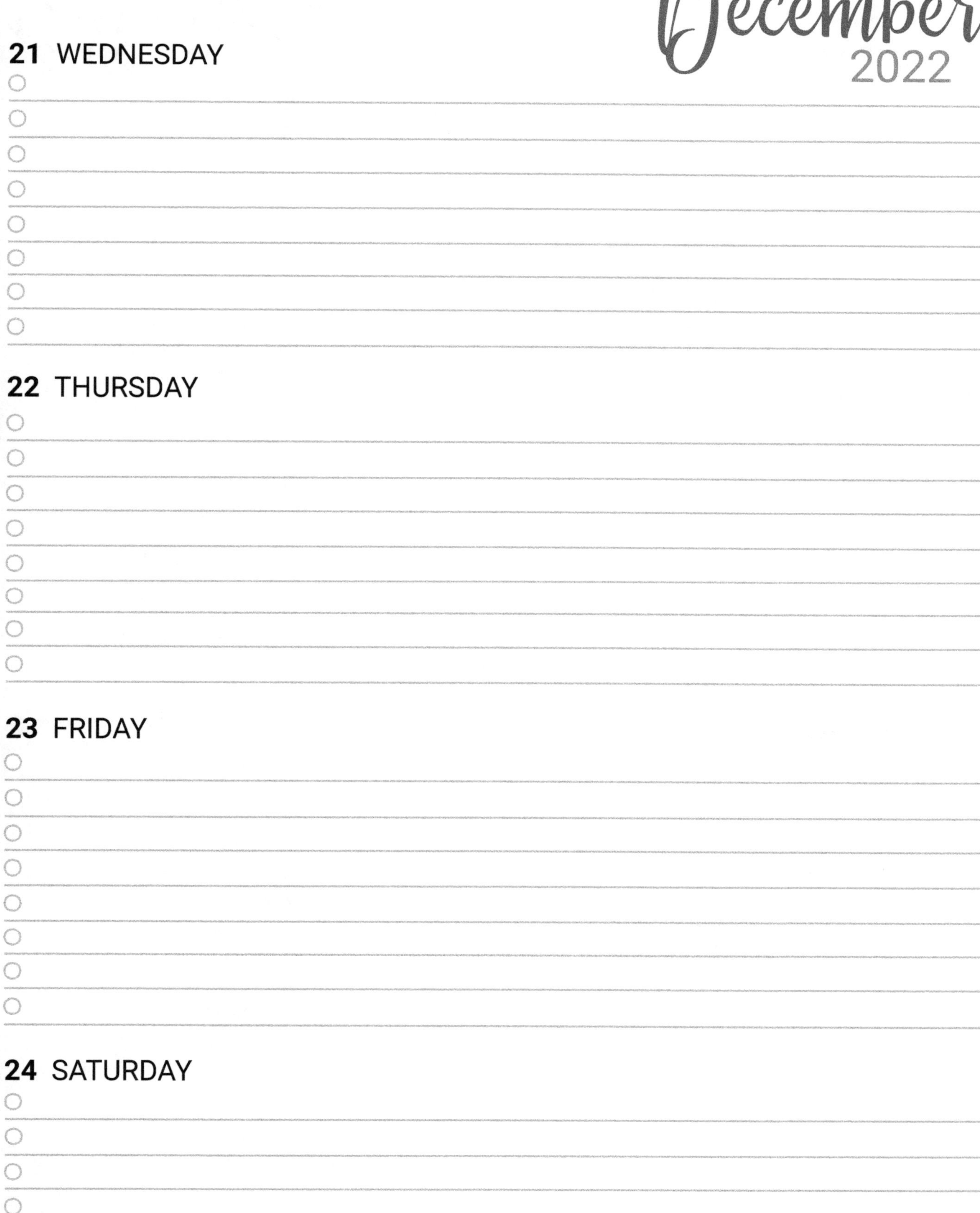

21 WEDNESDAY

22 THURSDAY

23 FRIDAY

24 SATURDAY

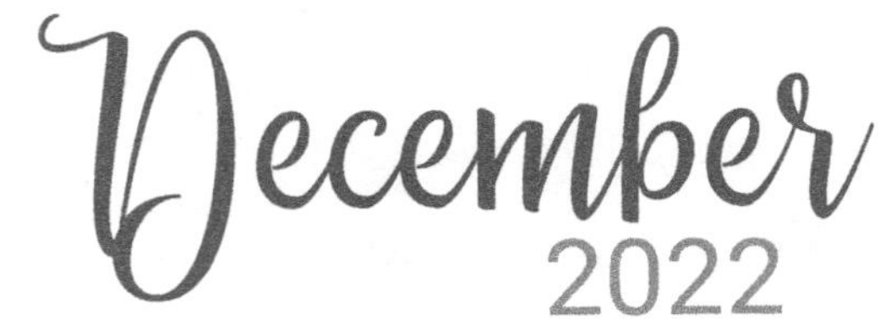

December
2022

25 SUNDAY

26 MONDAY

27 TUESDAY

28 WEDNESDAY

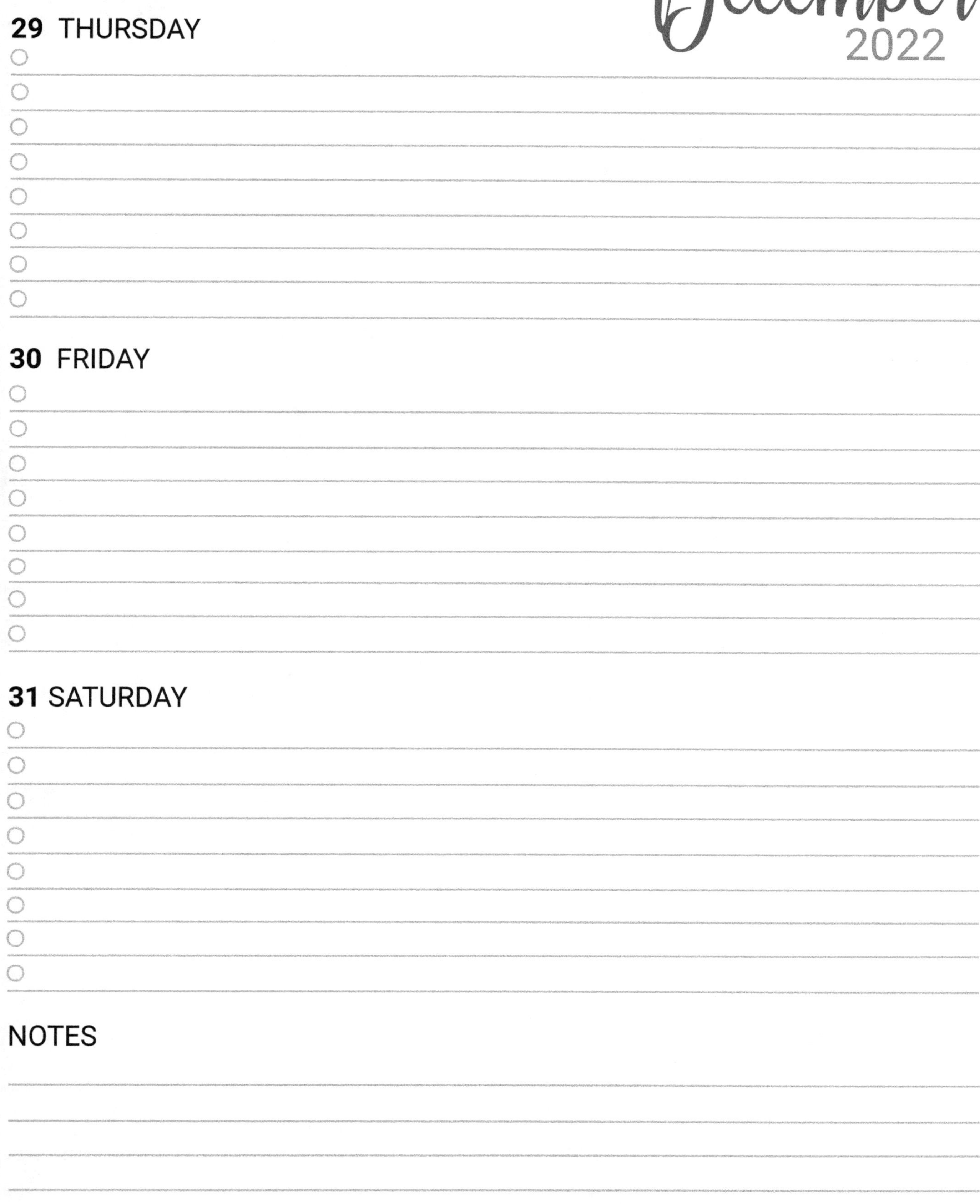

December
2022

29 THURSDAY

30 FRIDAY

31 SATURDAY

NOTES

01 SUNDAY

02 MONDAY

03 TUESDAY

04 WEDNESDAY

05 THURSDAY

06 FRIDAY

07 SATURDAY

08 SUNDAY

09 MONDAY

10 TUESDAY

11 WEDNESDAY

12 THURSDAY

13 FRIDAY

14 SATURDAY

15 SUNDAY

16 MONDAY

17 TUESDAY

18 WEDNESDAY

19 THURSDAY

20 FRIDAY

21 SATURDAY

22 SUNDAY

23 MONDAY

24 TUESDAY

25 WEDNESDAY

26 THURSDAY

27 FRIDAY

28 SATURDAY

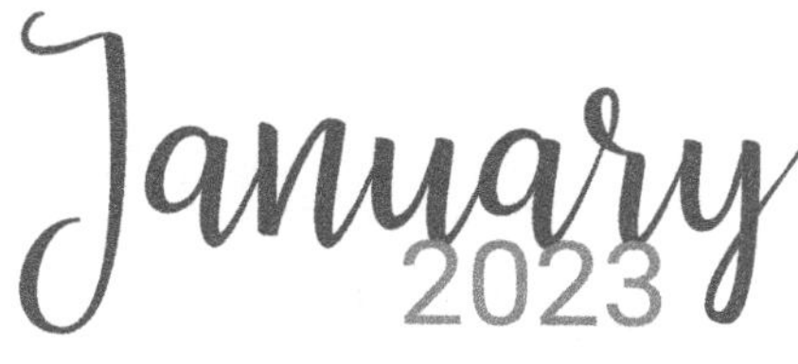

29 SUNDAY

30 MONDAY

31 TUESDAY

NOTES

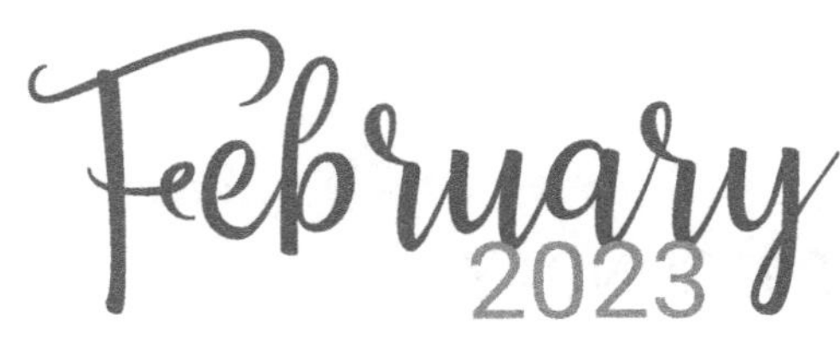

February
2023

01 WEDNESDAY

02 THURSDAY

03 FRIDAY

04 SATURDAY

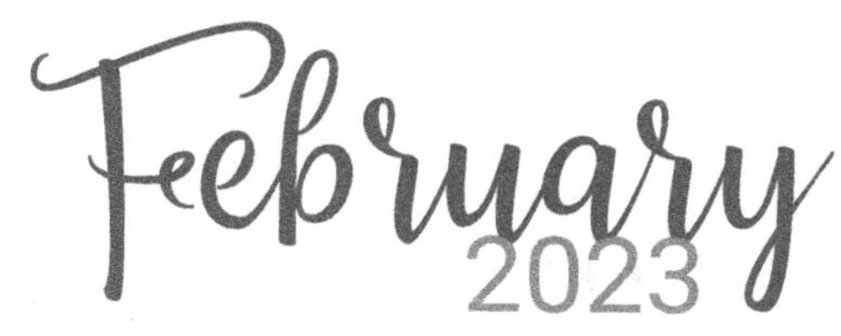

05 SUNDAY

06 MONDAY

07 TUESDAY

08 WEDNESDAY

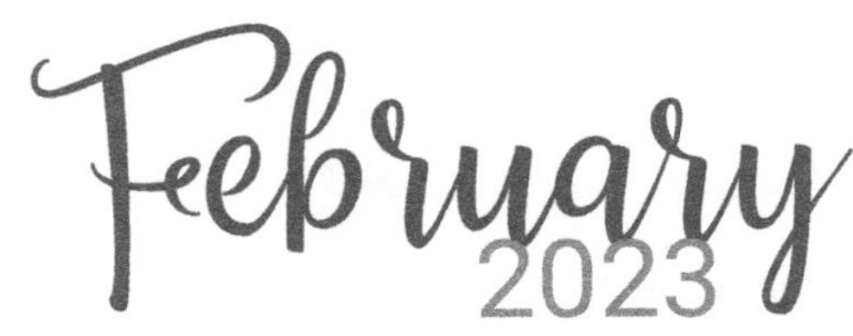

February 2023

09 THURSDAY

10 FRIDAY

11 SATURDAY

12 SUNDAY

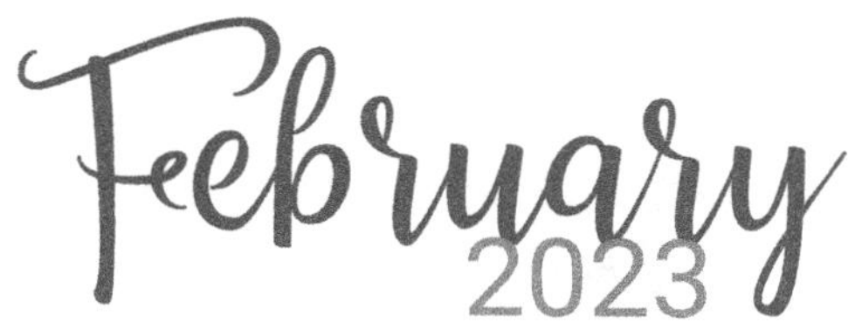

13 MONDAY

14 TUESDAY

15 WEDNESDAY

16 THURSDAY

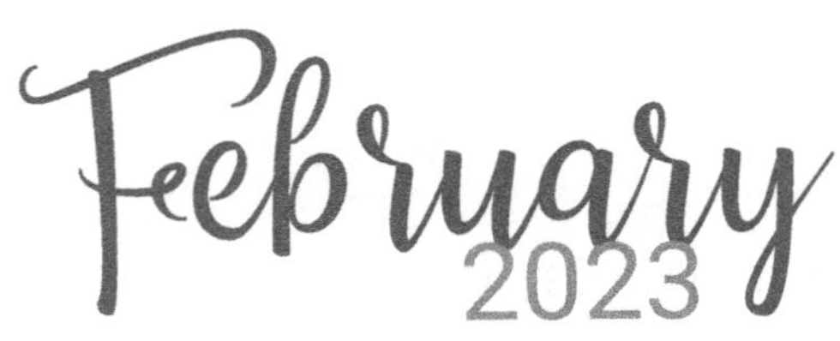

17 FRIDAY

18 SATURDAY

19 SUNDAY

20 MONDAY

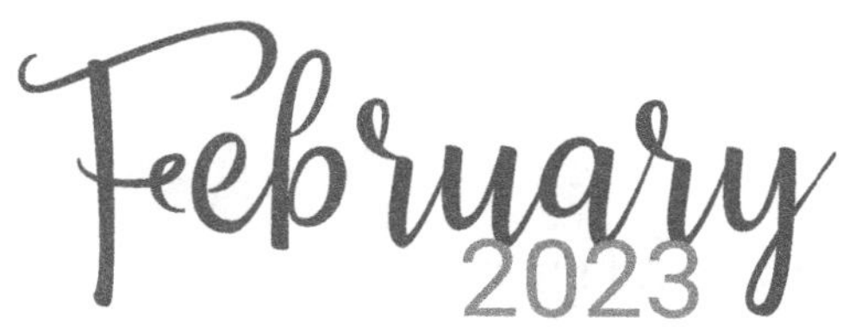

21 TUESDAY

22 WEDNESDAY

23 THURSDAY

24 FRIDAY

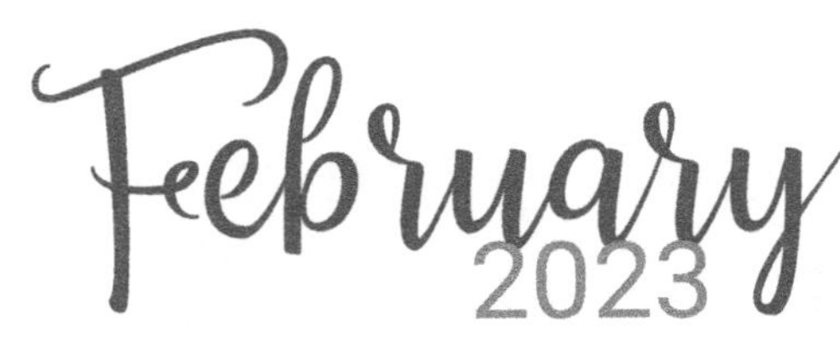

25 SATURDAY

26 SUNDAY

27 MONDAY

28 TUESDAY

01 WEDNESDAY

○
○
○
○
○
○
○
○

02 THURSDAY

○
○
○
○
○
○
○
○

03 FRIDAY

○
○
○
○
○
○
○
○

04 SATURDAY

○
○
○
○

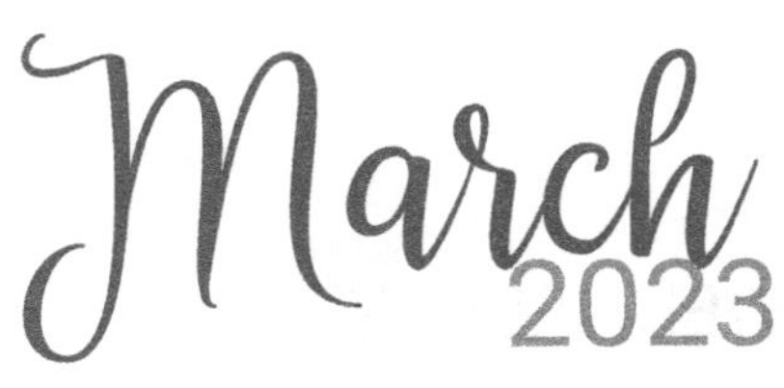

05 SUNDAY

06 MONDAY

07 TUESDAY

08 WEDNESDAY

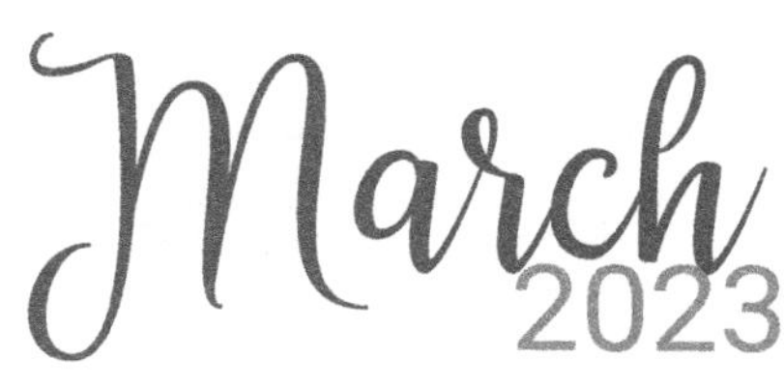

09 THURSDAY

10 FRIDAY

11 SATURDAY

12 SUNDAY

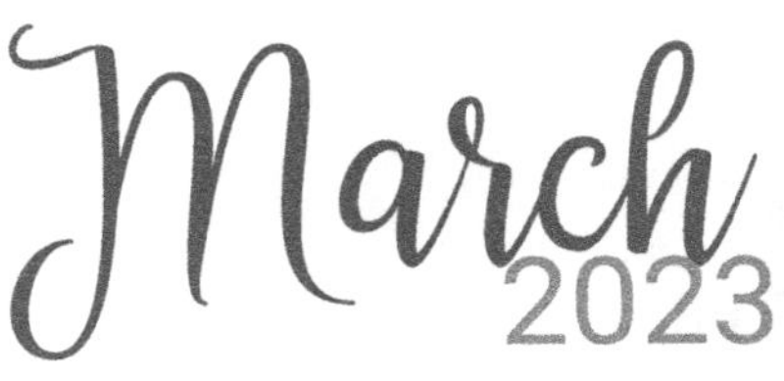

13 MONDAY

14 TUESDAY

15 WEDNESDAY

16 THURSDAY

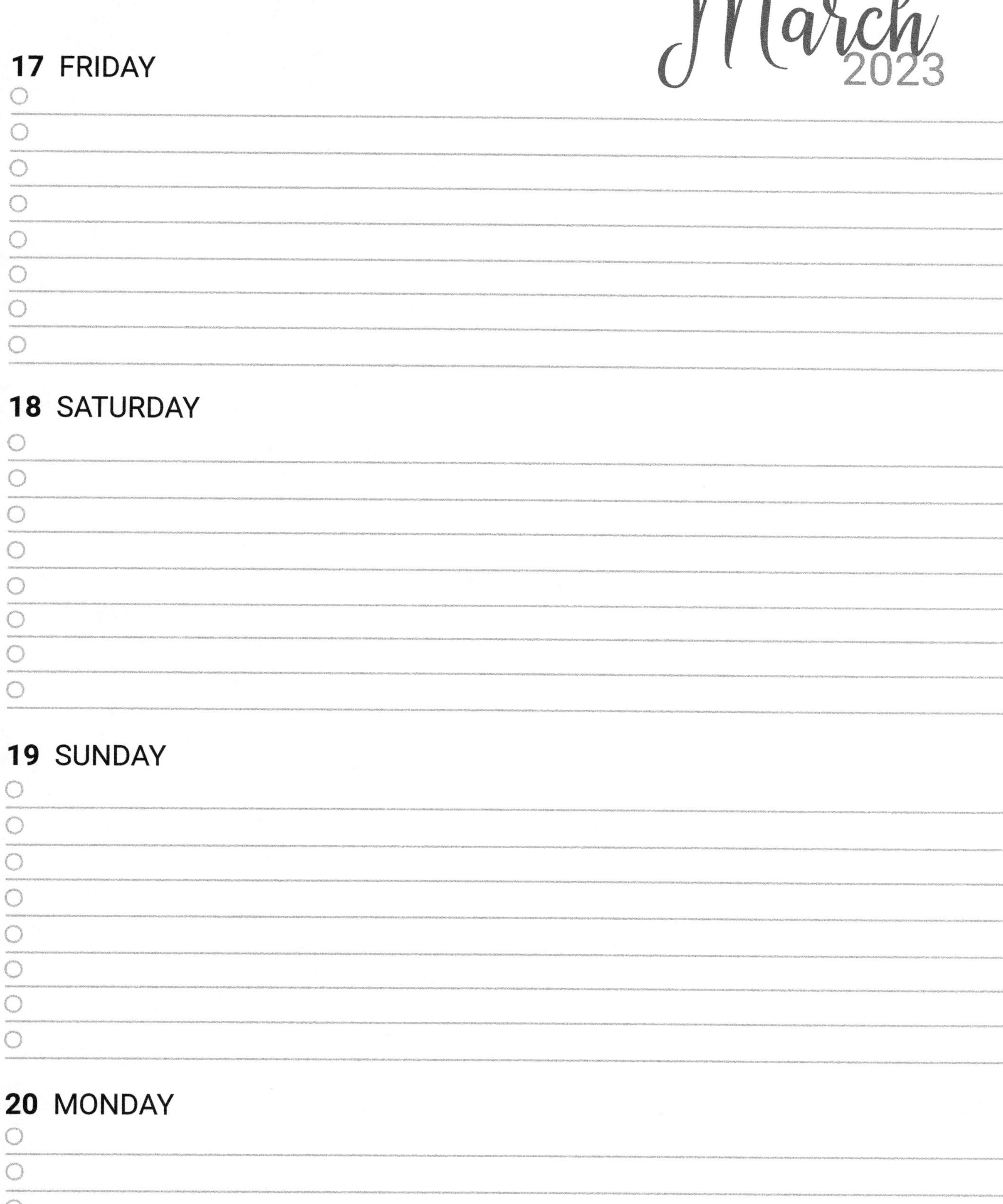

March
2023

17 FRIDAY

18 SATURDAY

19 SUNDAY

20 MONDAY

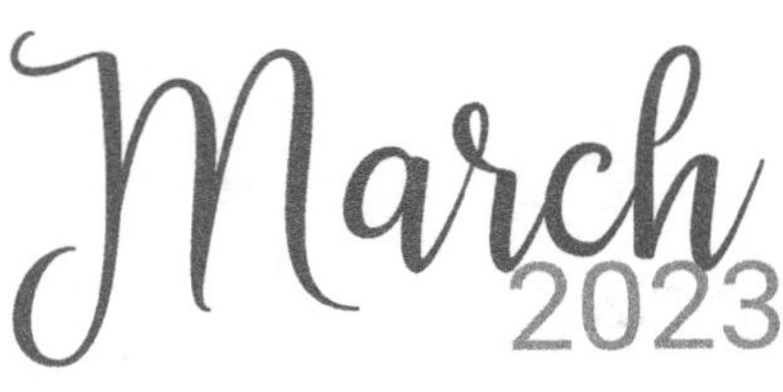

21 TUESDAY

22 WEDNESDAY

23 THURSDAY

24 FRIDAY

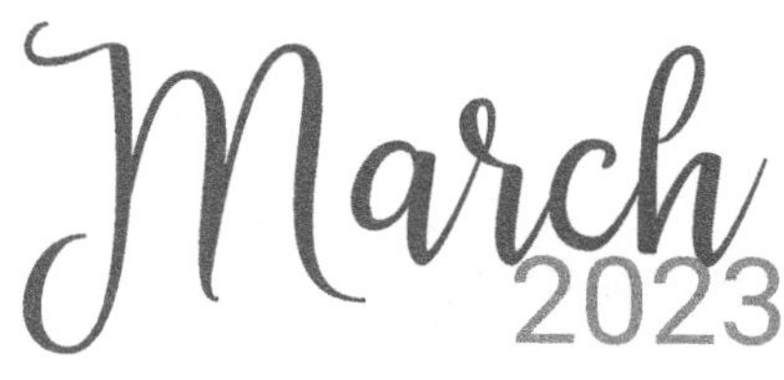

25 SATURDAY

26 SUNDAY

27 MONDAY

28 TUESDAY

29 WEDNESDAY

30 THURSDAY

31 FRIDAY

NOTES

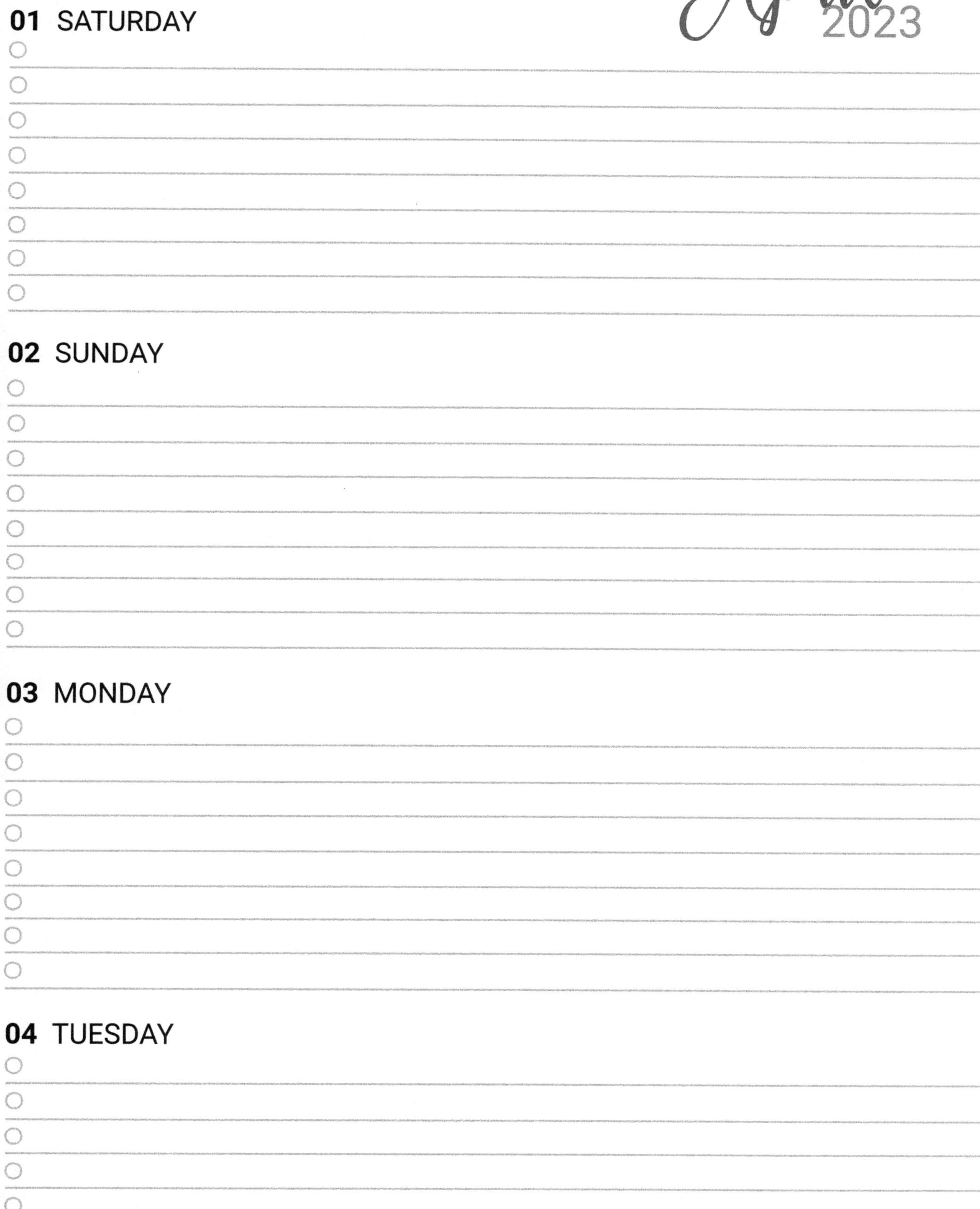

April
2023

01 SATURDAY

02 SUNDAY

03 MONDAY

04 TUESDAY

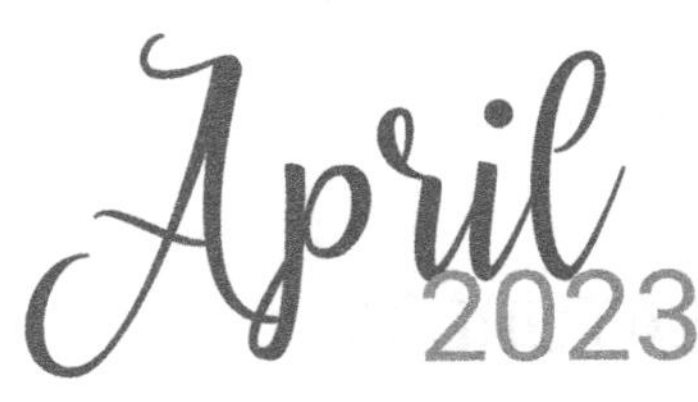

05 WEDNESDAY

06 THURSDAY

07 FRIDAY

08 SATURDAY

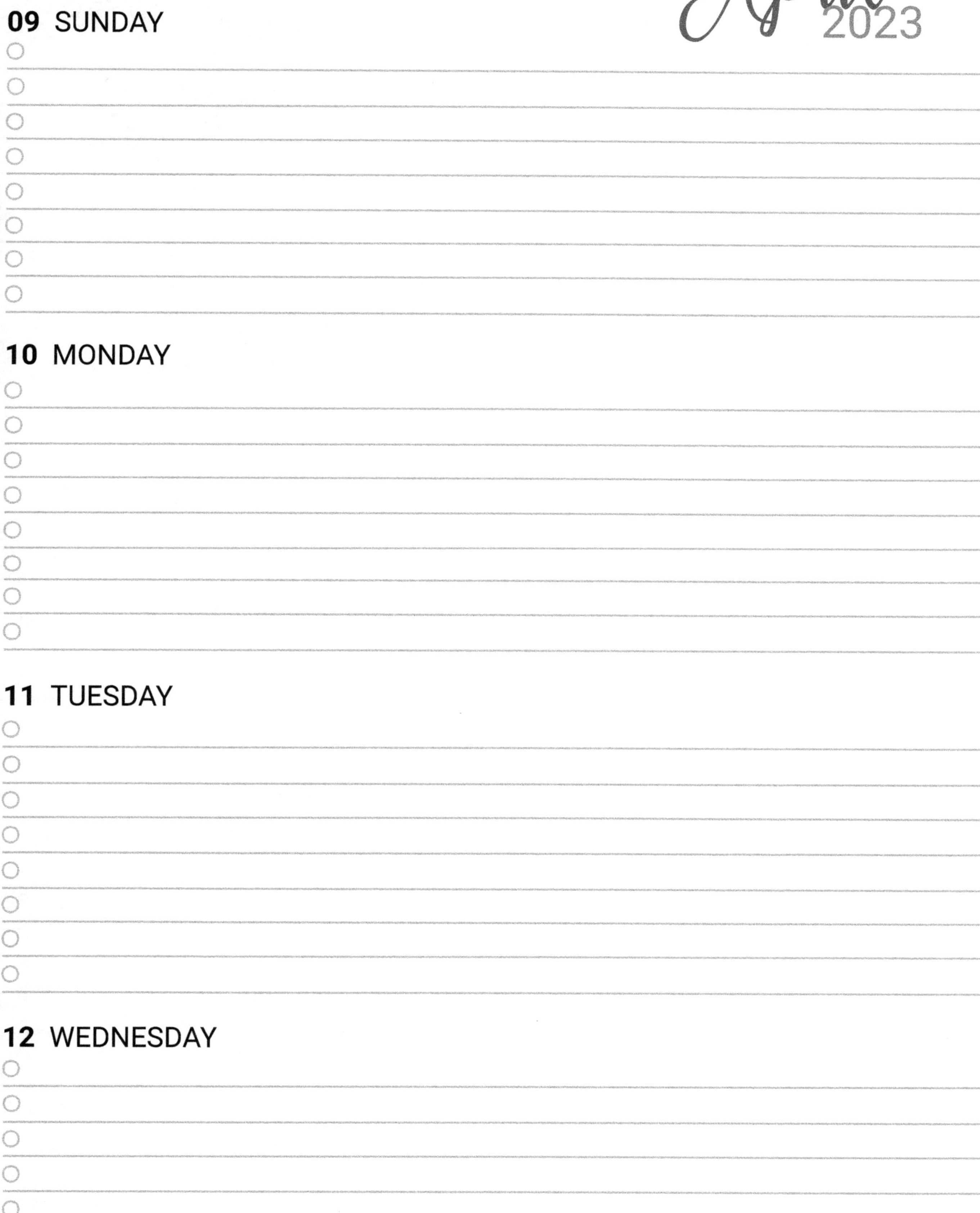

09 SUNDAY

10 MONDAY

11 TUESDAY

12 WEDNESDAY

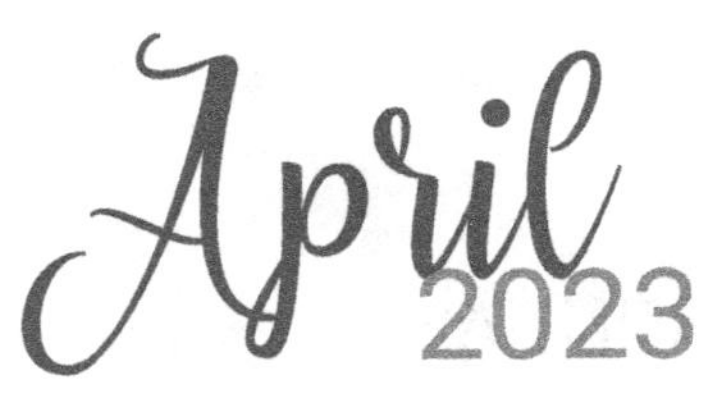

April 2023

13 THURSDAY

14 FRIDAY

15 SATURDAY

16 SUNDAY

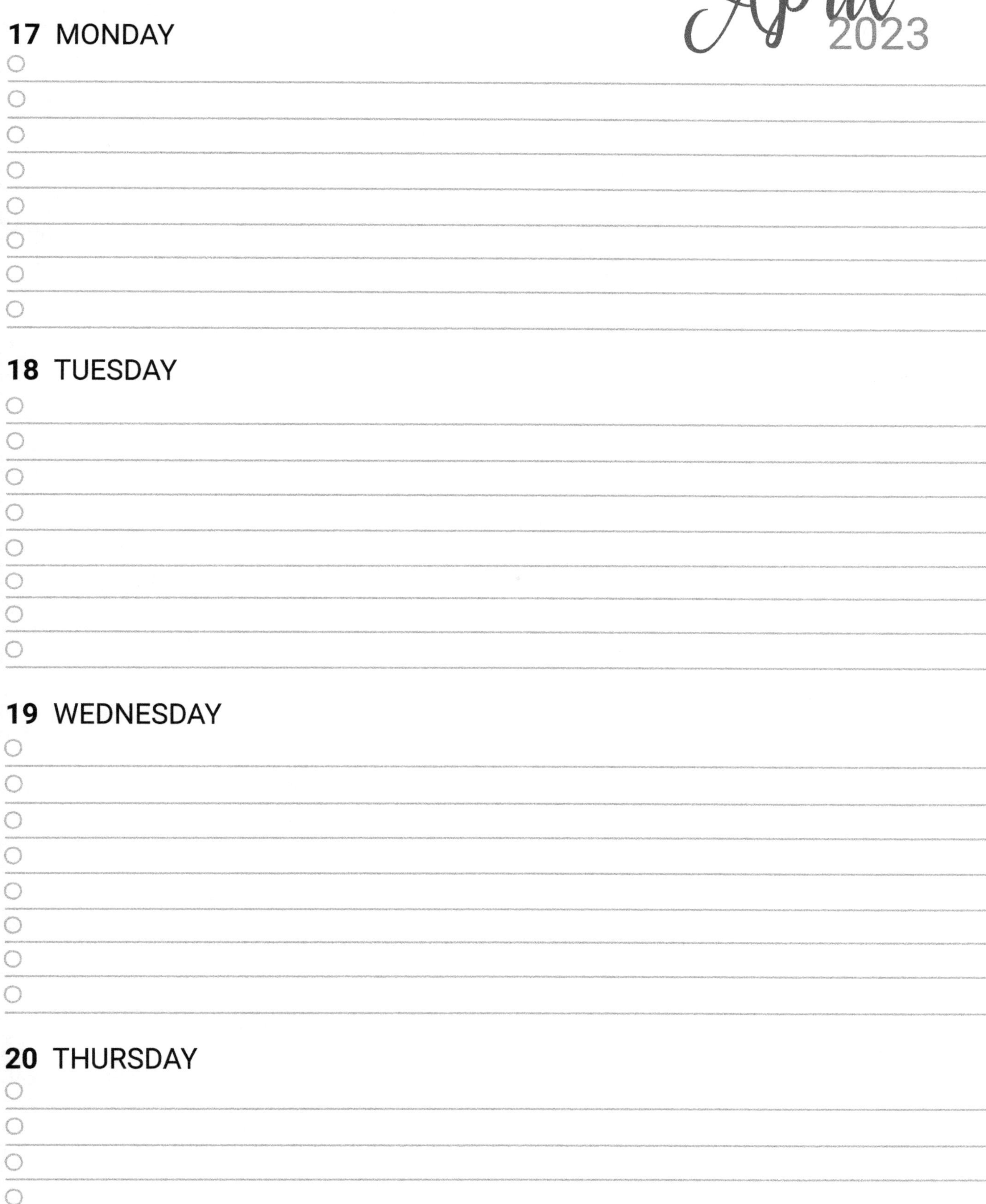

17 MONDAY

18 TUESDAY

19 WEDNESDAY

20 THURSDAY

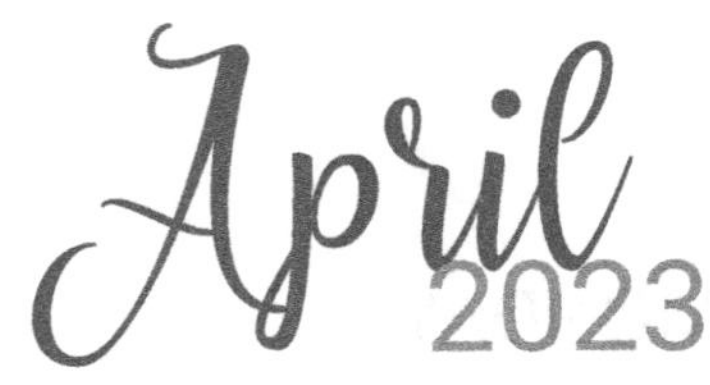

21 FRIDAY

22 SATURDAY

23 SUNDAY

24 MONDAY

25 TUESDAY

26 WEDNESDAY

27 THURSDAY

28 FRIDAY

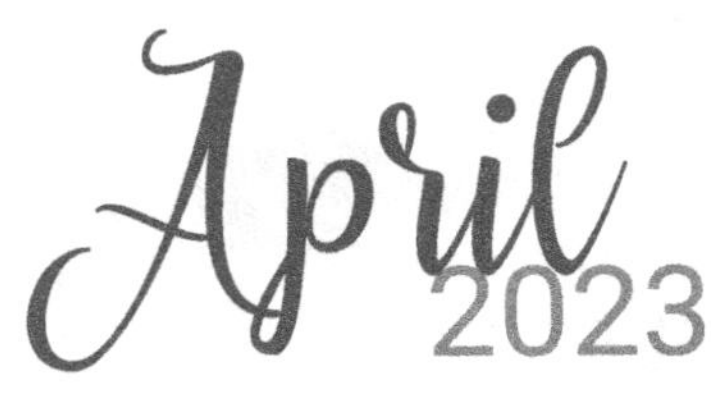

29 SATURDAY

30 SUNDAY

NOTES

01 MONDAY

02 TUESDAY

03 WEDNESDAY

04 THURSDAY

May
2023

05 FRIDAY

- ○
- ○
- ○
- ○
- ○
- ○
- ○
- ○

06 SATURDAY

- ○
- ○
- ○
- ○
- ○
- ○
- ○
- ○

07 SUNDAY

- ○
- ○
- ○
- ○
- ○
- ○
- ○
- ○

08 MONDAY

- ○
- ○
- ○
- ○
- ○

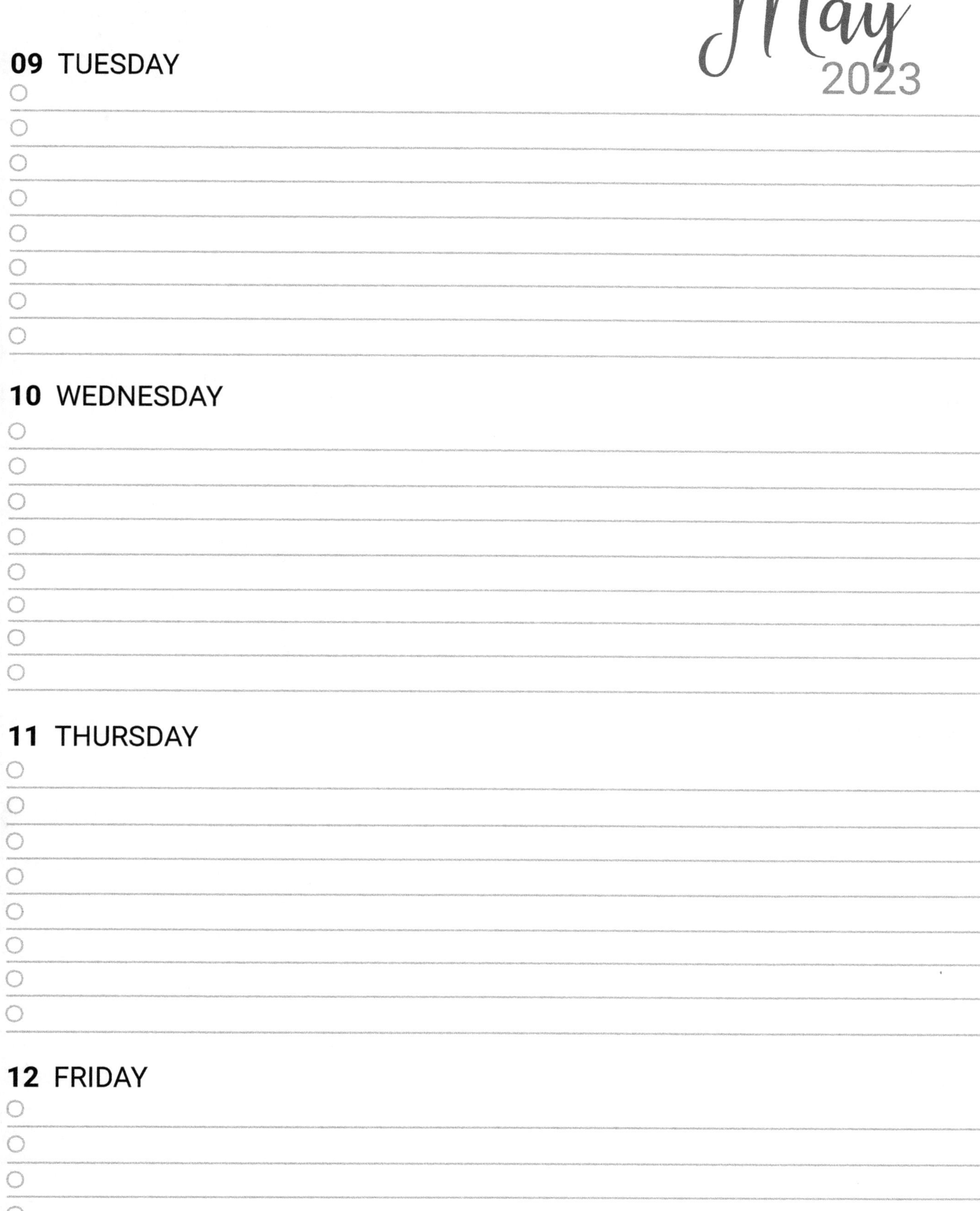

May 2023

09 TUESDAY

10 WEDNESDAY

11 THURSDAY

12 FRIDAY

13 SATURDAY

14 SUNDAY

15 MONDAY

16 TUESDAY

May
2023

17 WEDNESDAY

18 THURSDAY

19 FRIDAY

20 SATURDAY

21 SUNDAY

22 MONDAY

23 TUESDAY

24 WEDNESDAY

May
2023

25 THURSDAY

26 FRIDAY

27 SATURDAY

28 SUNDAY

29 MONDAY

30 TUESDAY

31 WEDNESDAY

NOTES

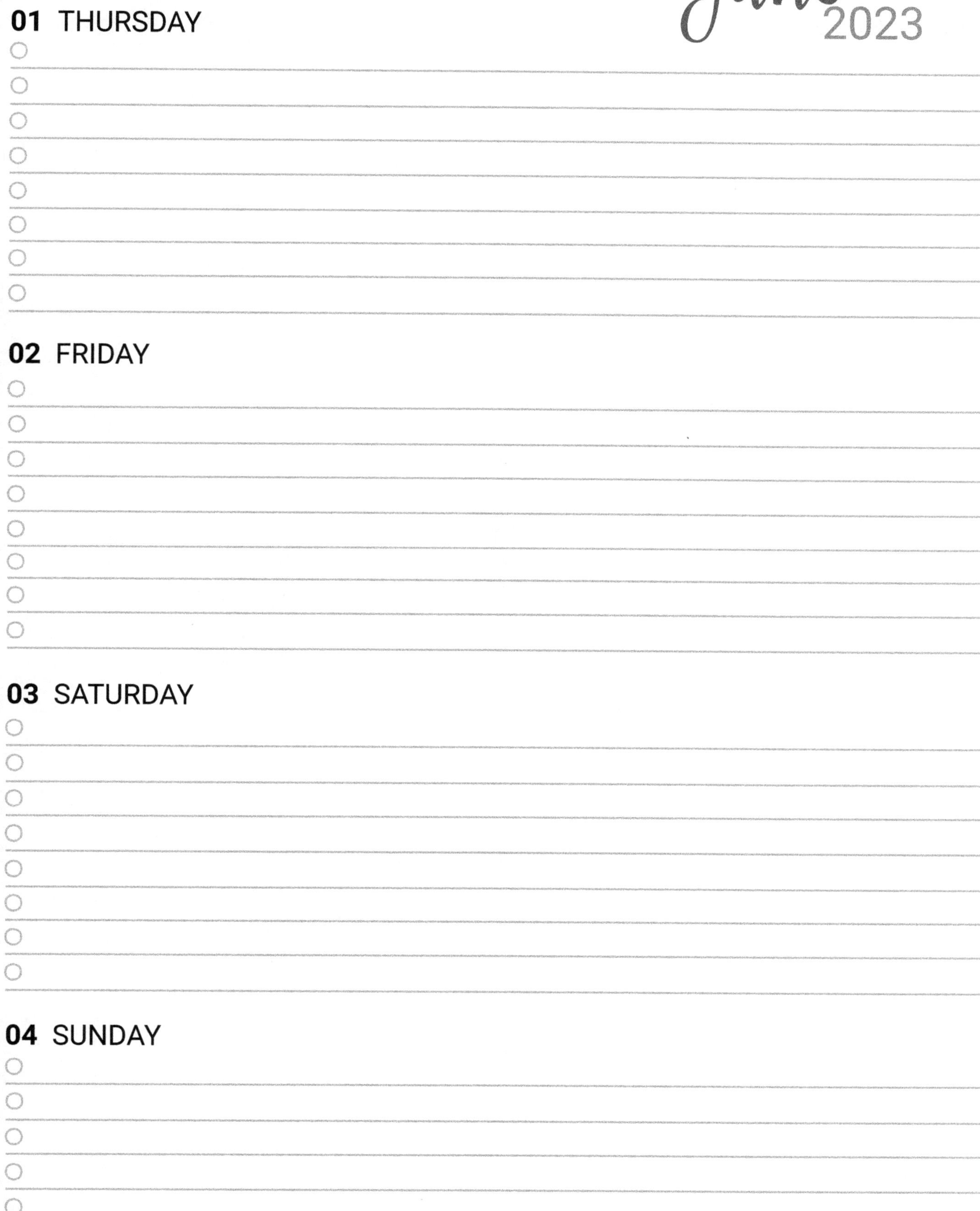
June
2023
01 THURSDAY
02 FRIDAY
03 SATURDAY
04 SUNDAY

05 MONDAY

06 TUESDAY

07 WEDNESDAY

08 THURSDAY

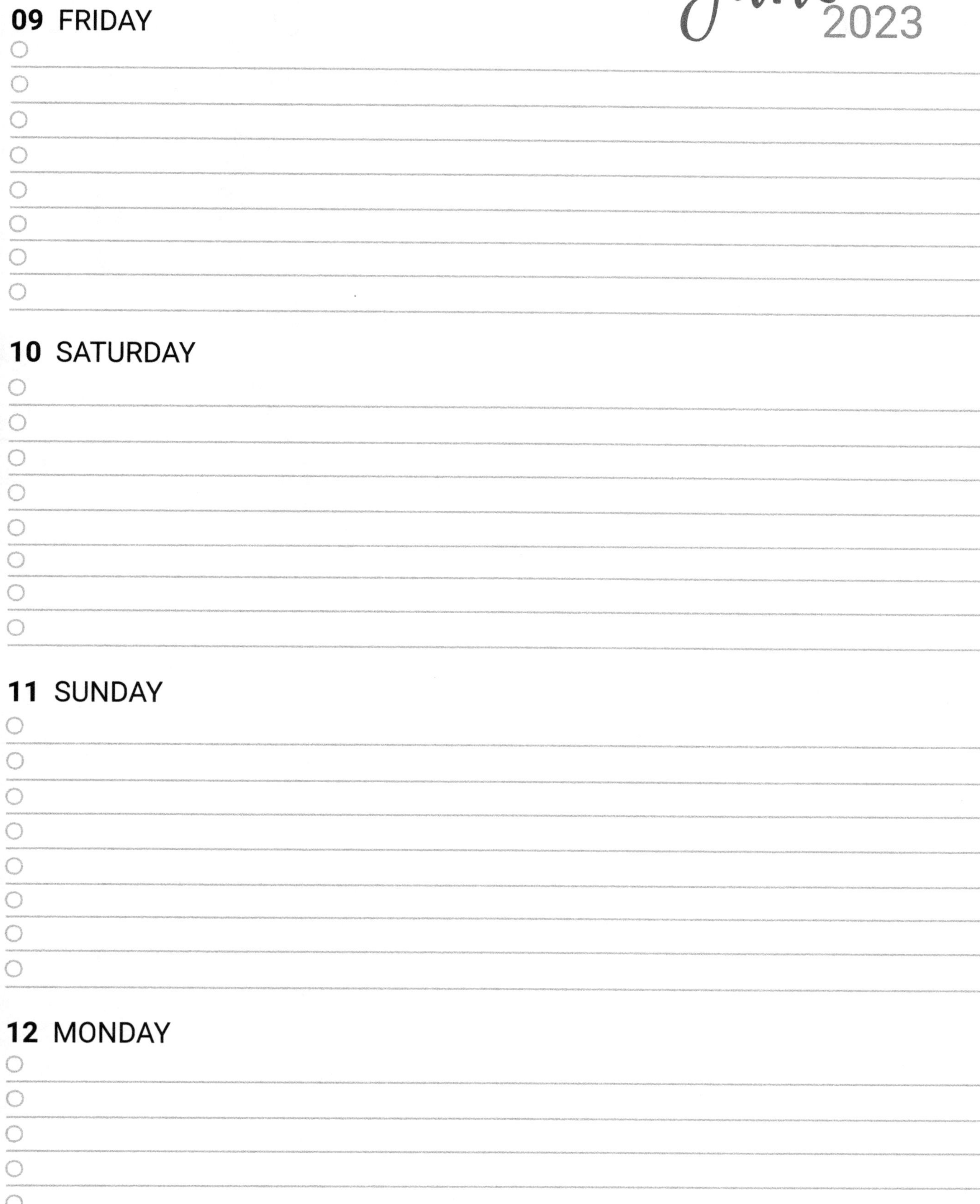

June
2023

09 FRIDAY

10 SATURDAY

11 SUNDAY

12 MONDAY

13 TUESDAY

14 WEDNESDAY

15 THURSDAY

16 FRIDAY

June
2023

17 SATURDAY

○
○
○
○
○
○
○

18 SUNDAY

○
○
○
○
○
○
○

19 MONDAY

○
○
○
○
○
○
○

20 TUESDAY

○
○
○
○
○

21 WEDNESDAY

22 THURSDAY

23 FRIDAY

24 SATURDAY

25 SUNDAY

○ ____________________
○ ____________________
○ ____________________
○ ____________________
○ ____________________
○ ____________________
○ ____________________

26 MONDAY

○ ____________________
○ ____________________
○ ____________________
○ ____________________
○ ____________________
○ ____________________
○ ____________________
○ ____________________

27 TUESDAY

○ ____________________
○ ____________________
○ ____________________
○ ____________________
○ ____________________
○ ____________________
○ ____________________

28 WEDNESDAY

○ ____________________
○ ____________________
○ ____________________
○ ____________________

29 THURSDAY

30 FRIDAY

NOTES

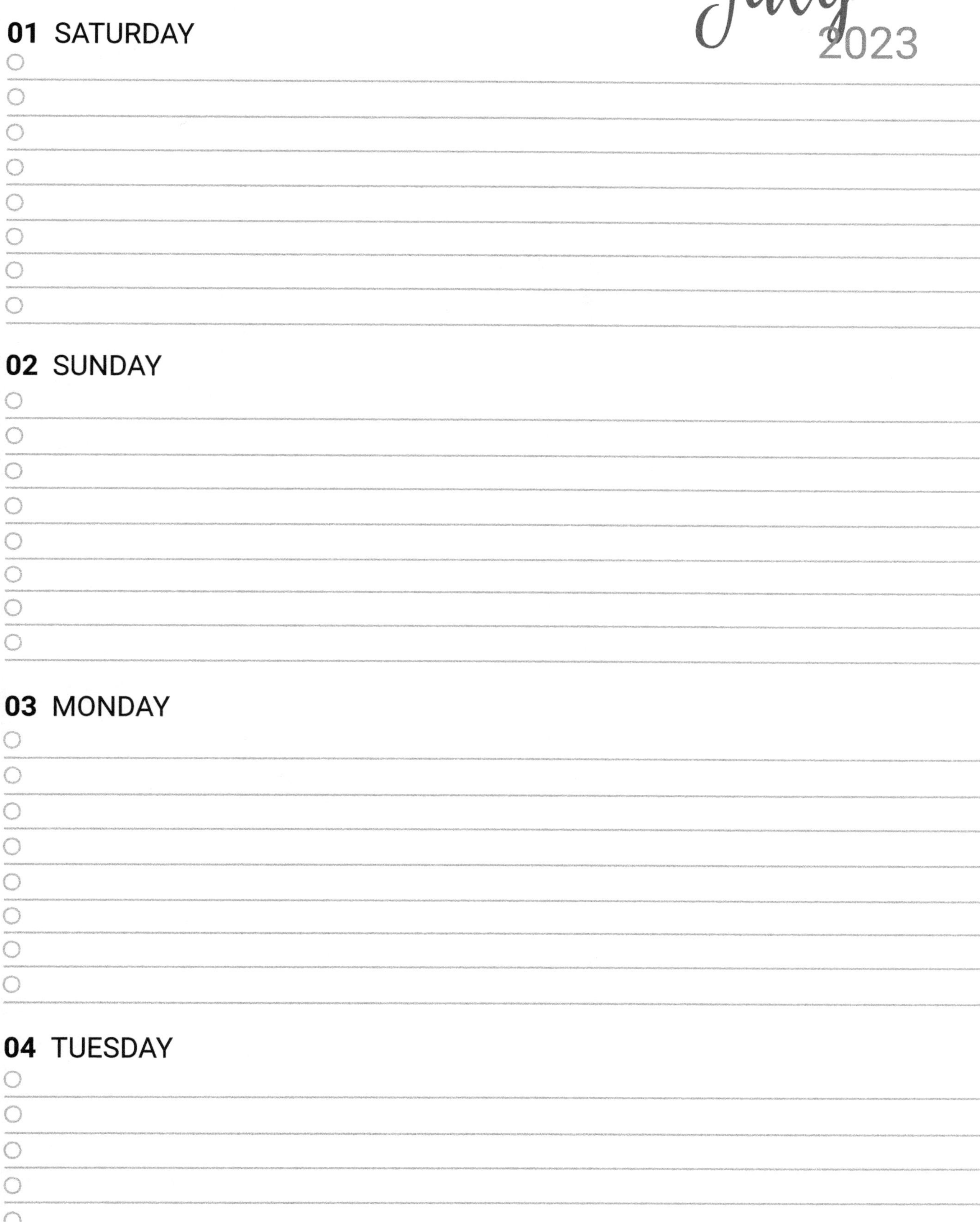

July
2023

01 SATURDAY

02 SUNDAY

03 MONDAY

04 TUESDAY

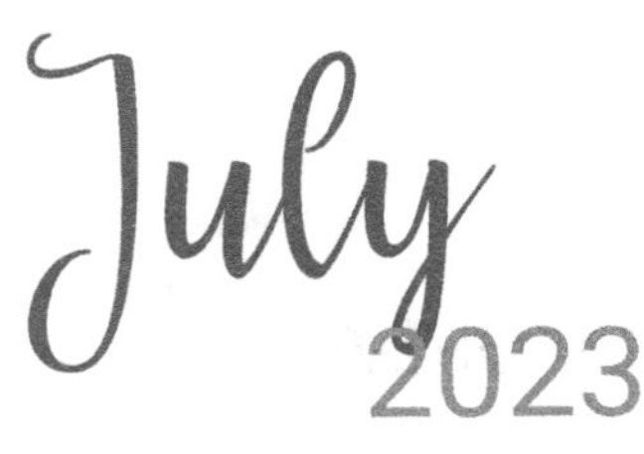

July
2023

05 WEDNESDAY

06 THURSDAY

07 FRIDAY

08 SATURDAY

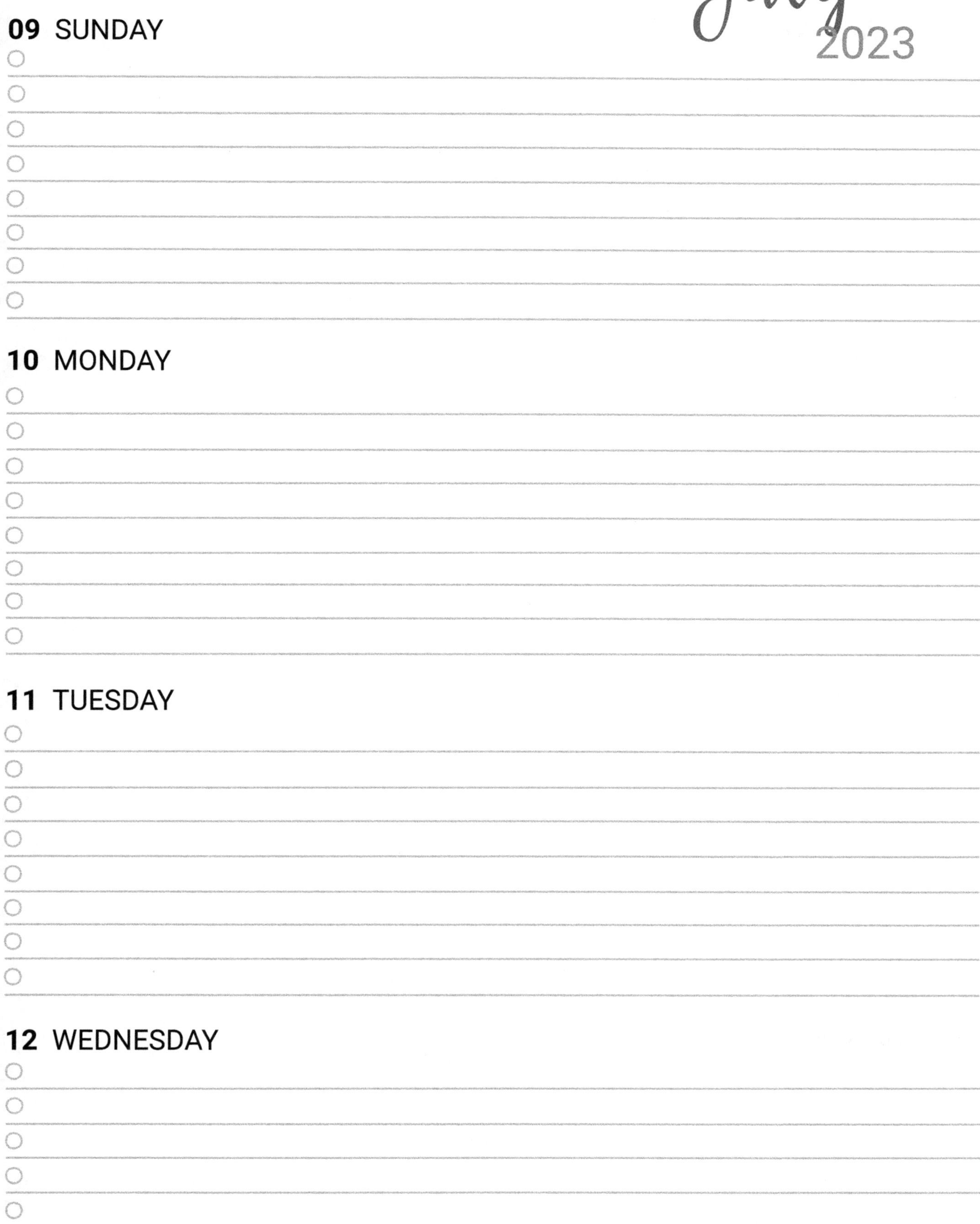

July
2023

09 SUNDAY

10 MONDAY

11 TUESDAY

12 WEDNESDAY

July
2023

13 THURSDAY

14 FRIDAY

15 SATURDAY

16 SUNDAY

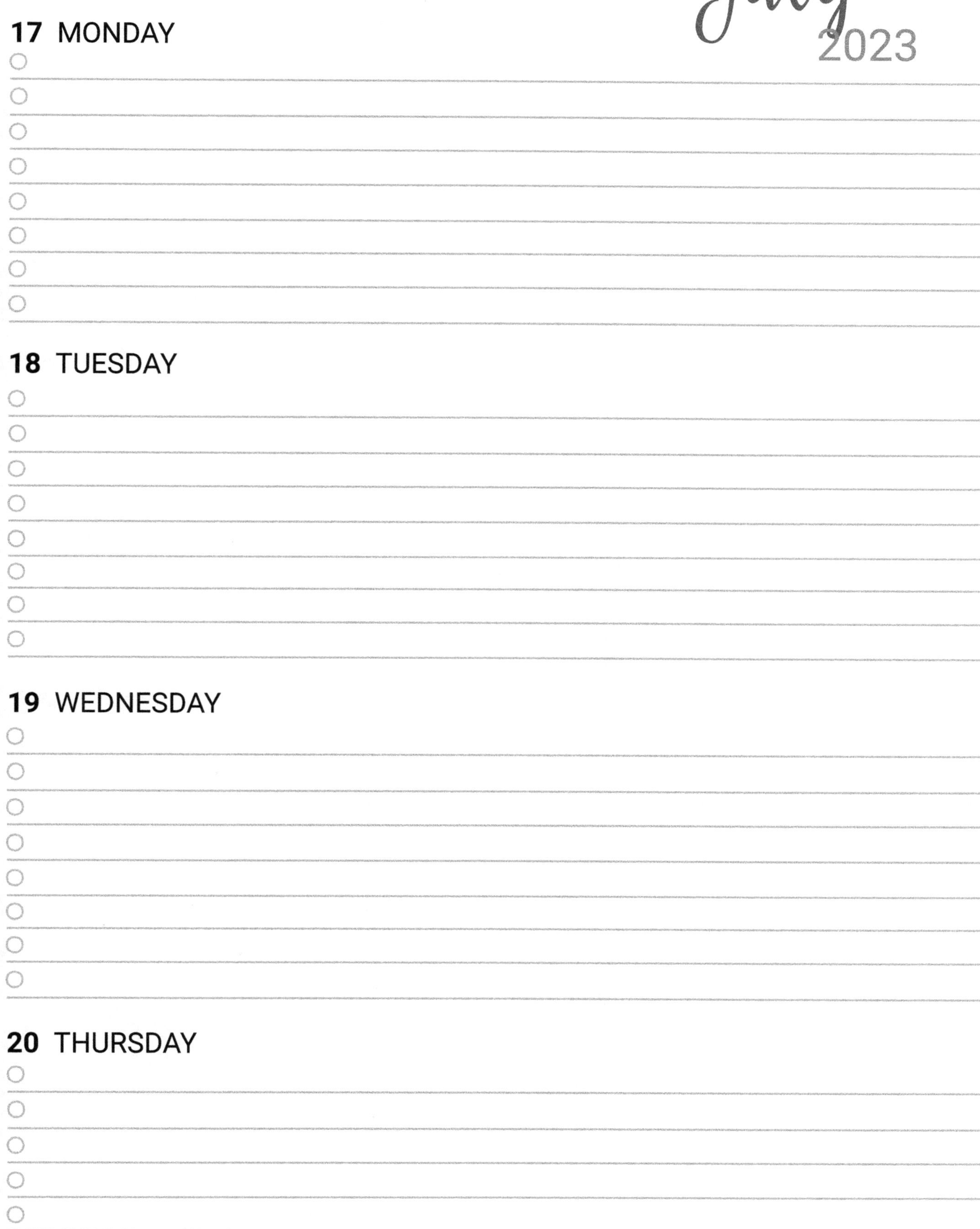

17 MONDAY

18 TUESDAY

19 WEDNESDAY

20 THURSDAY

21 FRIDAY

22 SATURDAY

23 SUNDAY

24 MONDAY

25 TUESDAY

26 WEDNESDAY

27 THURSDAY

28 FRIDAY

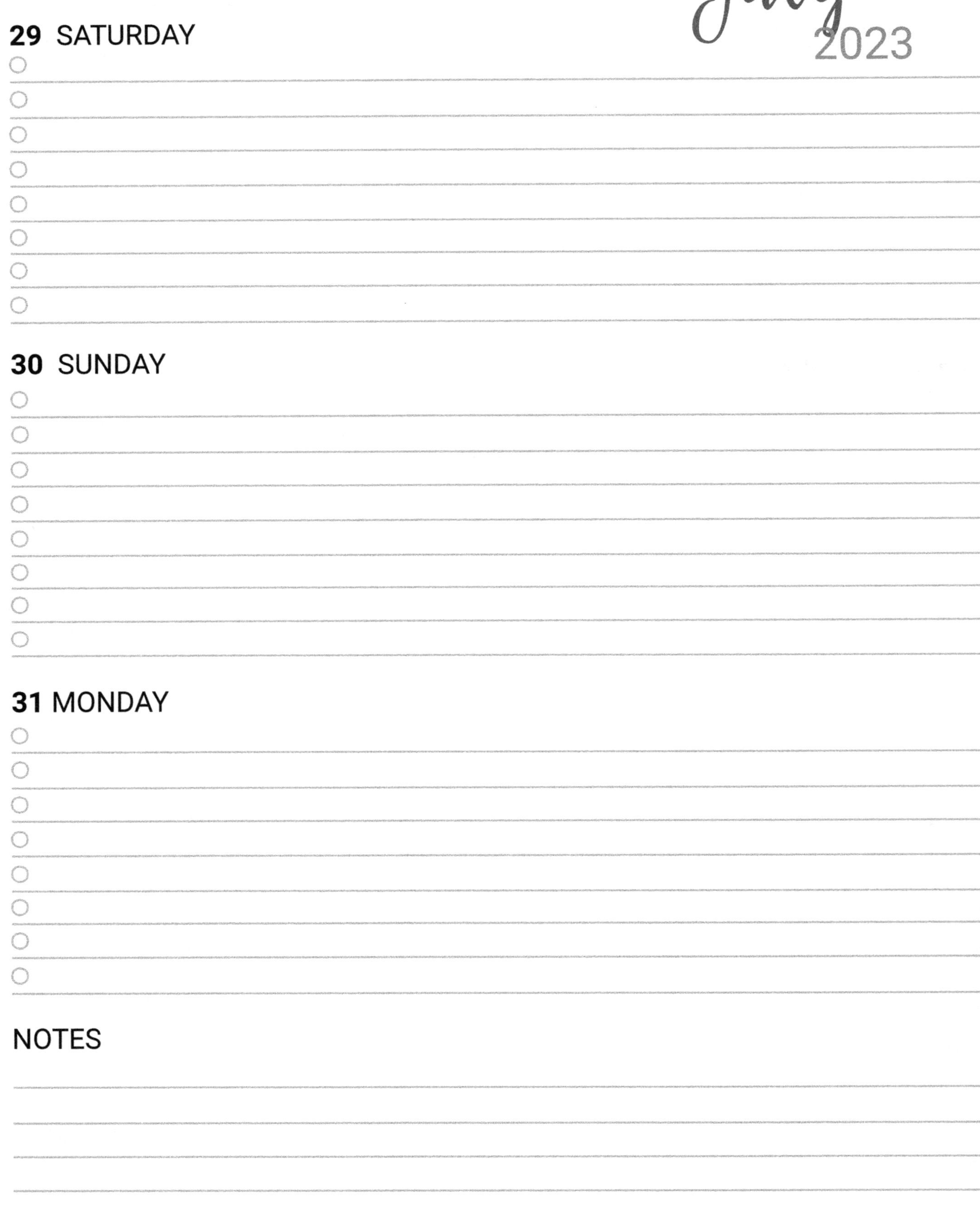

29 SATURDAY

30 SUNDAY

31 MONDAY

NOTES

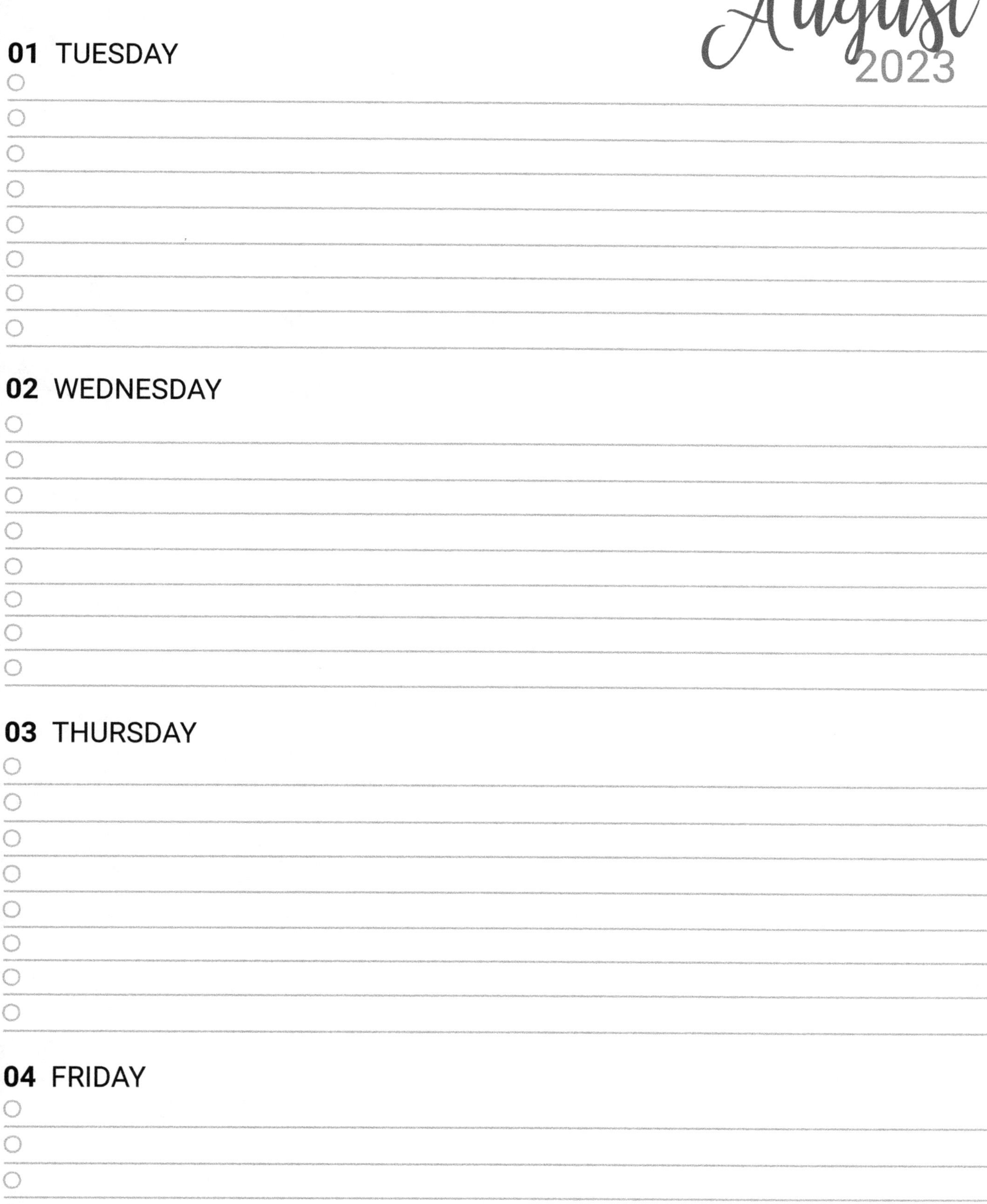

01 TUESDAY

02 WEDNESDAY

03 THURSDAY

04 FRIDAY

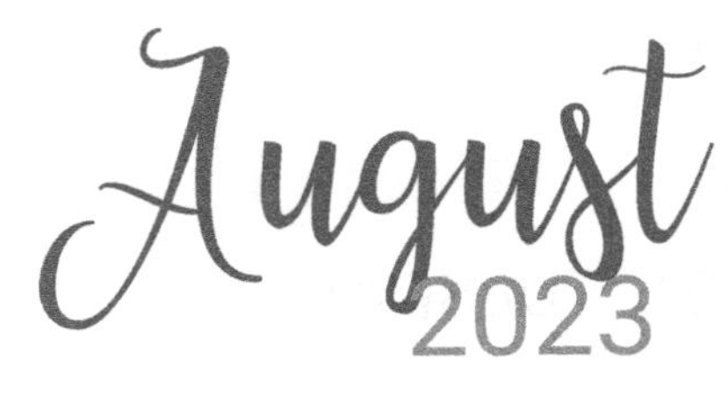

05 SATURDAY

06 SUNDAY

07 MONDAY

08 TUESDAY

09 WEDNESDAY

10 THURSDAY

11 FRIDAY

12 SATURDAY

13 SUNDAY

14 MONDAY

15 TUESDAY

16 WEDNESDAY

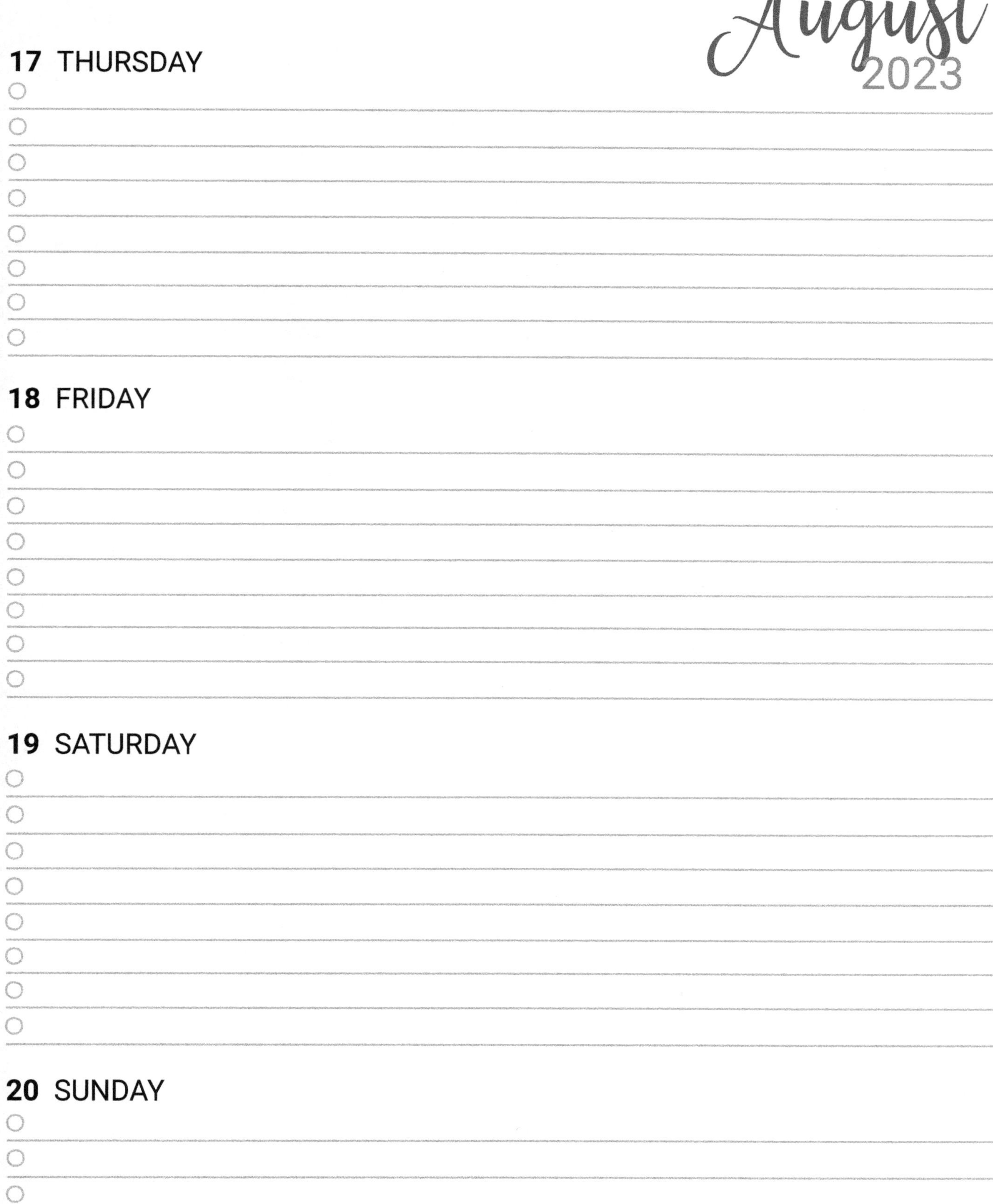

August
2023

17 THURSDAY

18 FRIDAY

19 SATURDAY

20 SUNDAY

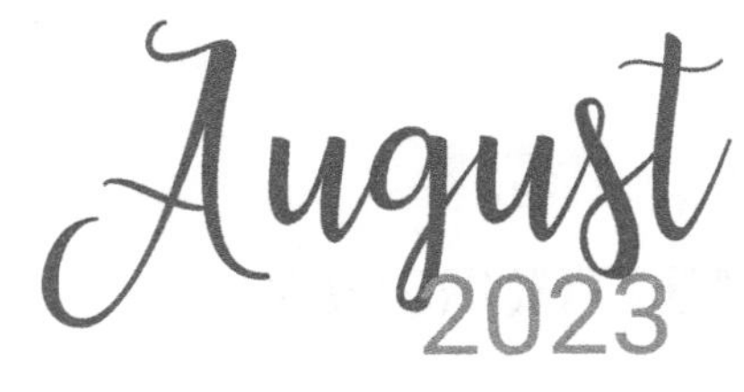

21 MONDAY

22 TUESDAY

23 WEDNESDAY

24 THURSDAY

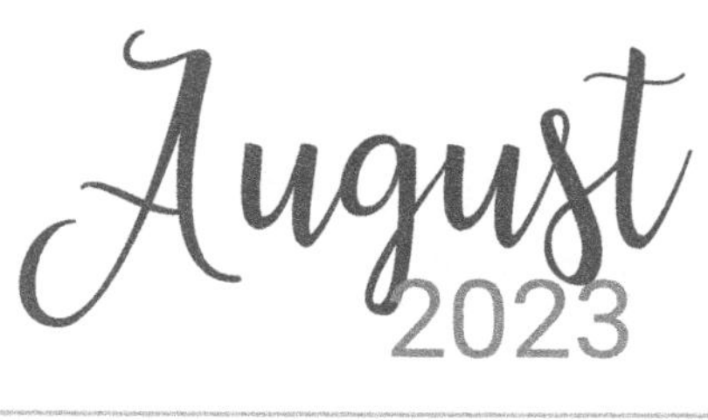

25 FRIDAY

26 SATURDAY

27 SUNDAY

28 MONDAY

29 TUESDAY

30 WEDNESDAY

31 THURSDAY

NOTES

01 FRIDAY

02 SATURDAY

03 SUNDAY

04 MONDAY

05 TUESDAY

06 WEDNESDAY

07 THURSDAY

08 FRIDAY

09 SATURDAY

10 SUNDAY

11 MONDAY

12 TUESDAY

13 WEDNESDAY

14 THURSDAY

15 FRIDAY

16 SATURDAY

17 SUNDAY

18 MONDAY

19 TUESDAY

20 WEDNESDAY

21 THURSDAY

22 FRIDAY

23 SATURDAY

24 SUNDAY

25 MONDAY

26 TUESDAY

27 WEDNESDAY

28 THURSDAY

29 FRIDAY

30 SATURDAY

NOTES

01 SUNDAY

02 MONDAY

03 TUESDAY

04 WEDNESDAY

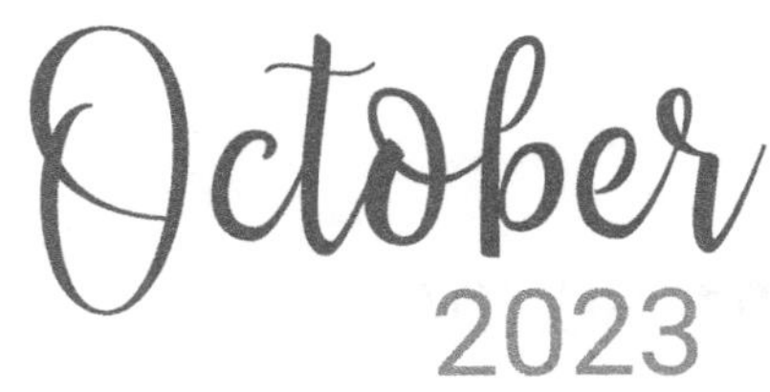

05 THURSDAY

○
○
○
○
○
○
○
○

06 FRIDAY

○
○
○
○
○
○
○
○

07 SATURDAY

○
○
○
○
○
○
○
○

08 SUNDAY

○
○
○
○
○

09 MONDAY

10 TUESDAY

11 WEDNESDAY

12 THURSDAY

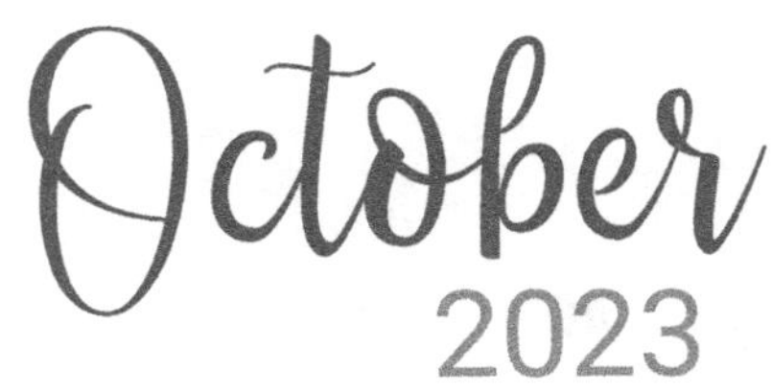

October
2023

13 FRIDAY

14 SATURDAY

15 SUNDAY

16 MONDAY

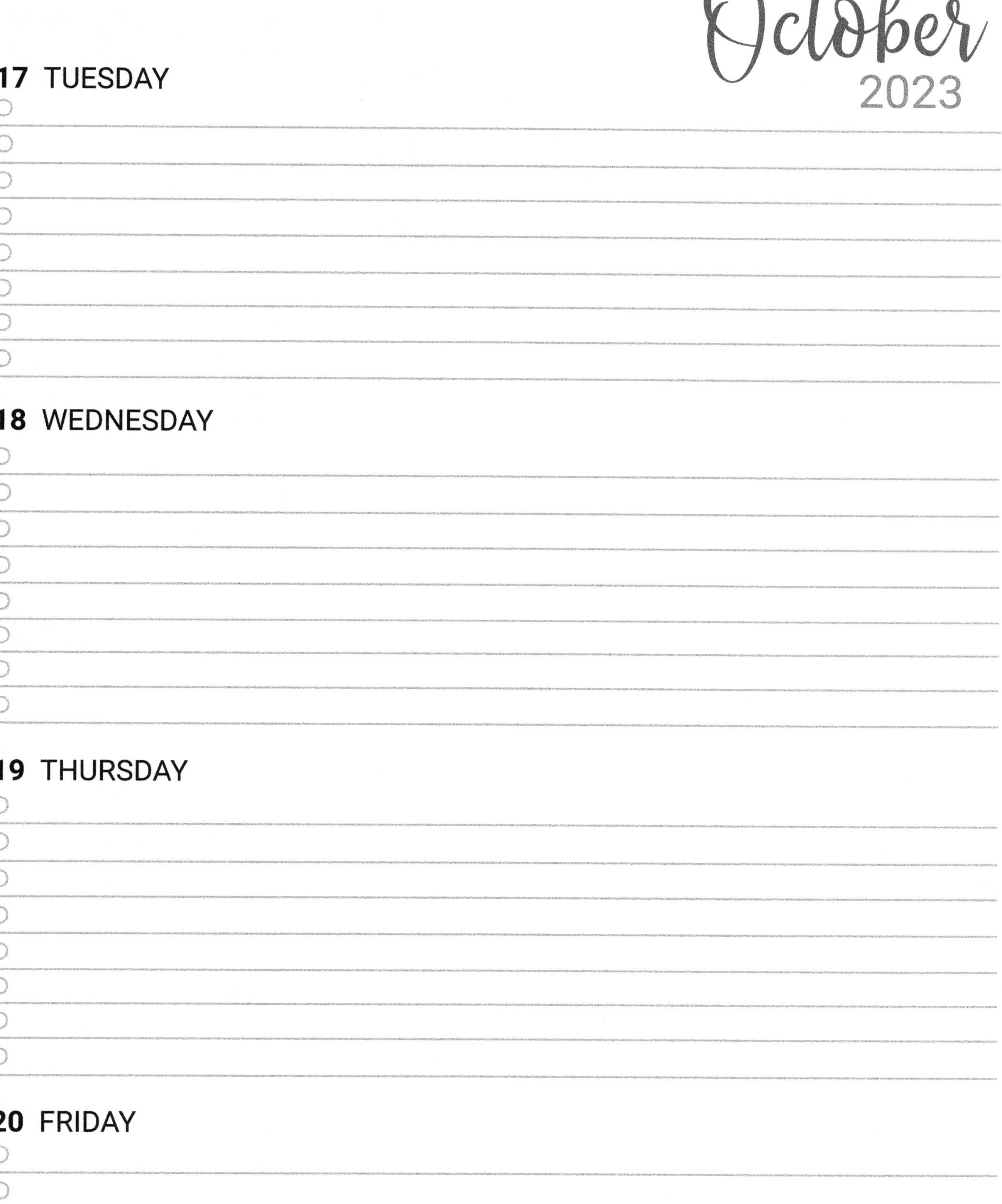

17 TUESDAY

18 WEDNESDAY

19 THURSDAY

20 FRIDAY

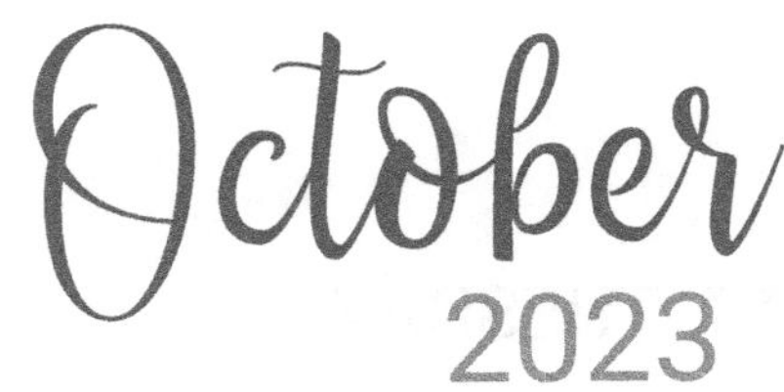

October
2023

21 SATURDAY

22 SUNDAY

23 MONDAY

24 TUESDAY

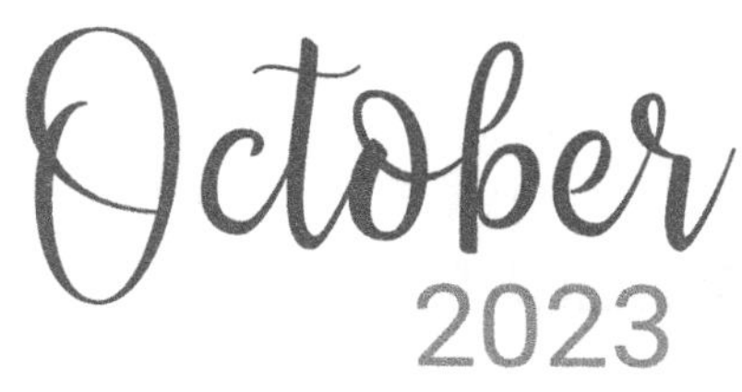

25 WEDNESDAY

26 THURSDAY

27 FRIDAY

28 SATURDAY

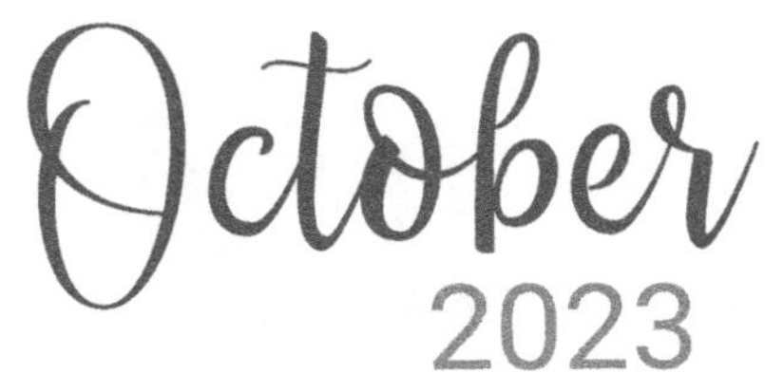

29 SUNDAY

30 MONDAY

31 TUESDAY

NOTES

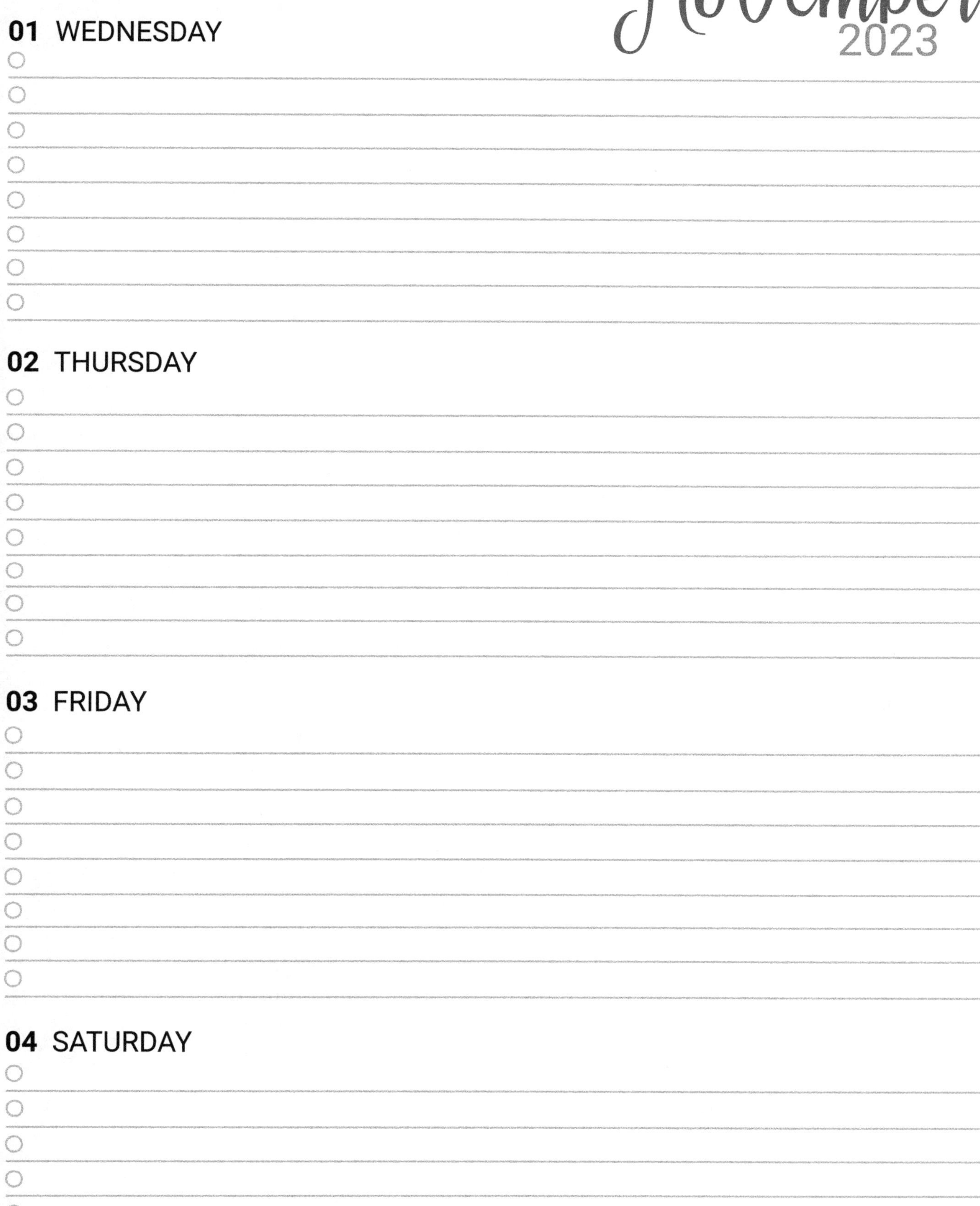

November
2023

01 WEDNESDAY

02 THURSDAY

03 FRIDAY

04 SATURDAY

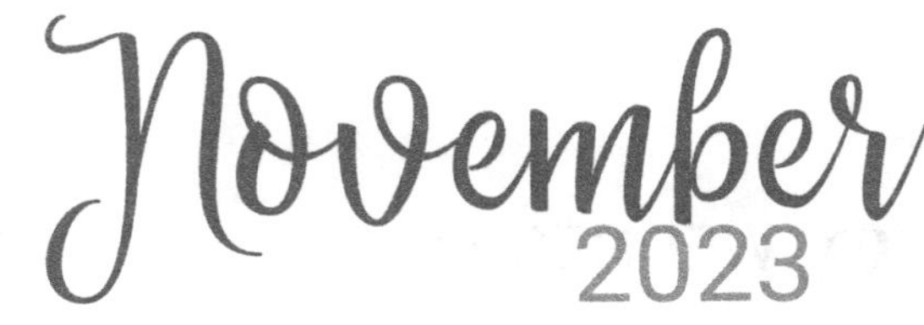

05 SUNDAY

06 MONDAY

07 TUESDAY

08 WEDNESDAY

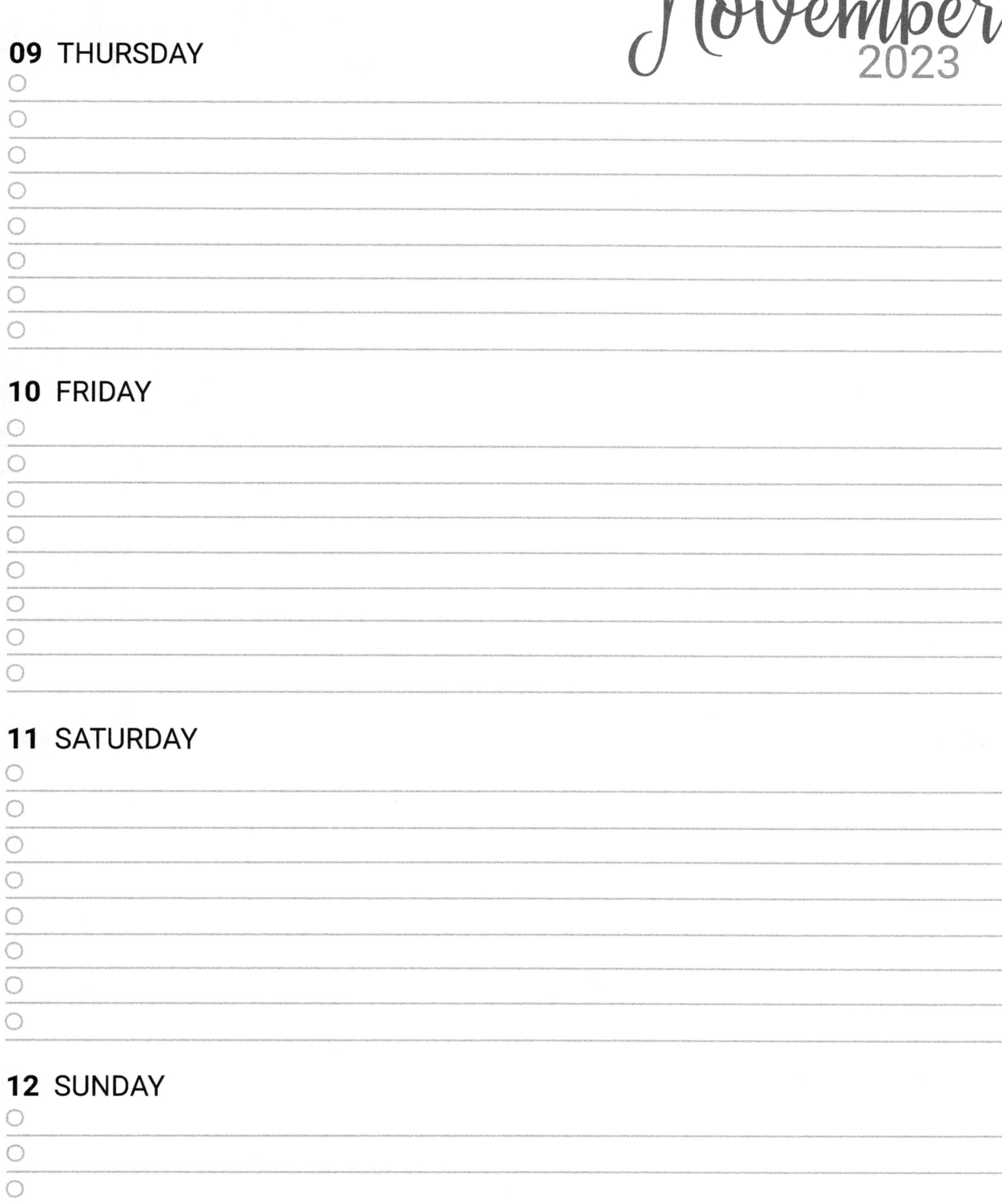

09 THURSDAY

10 FRIDAY

11 SATURDAY

12 SUNDAY

13 MONDAY

14 TUESDAY

15 WEDNESDAY

16 THURSDAY

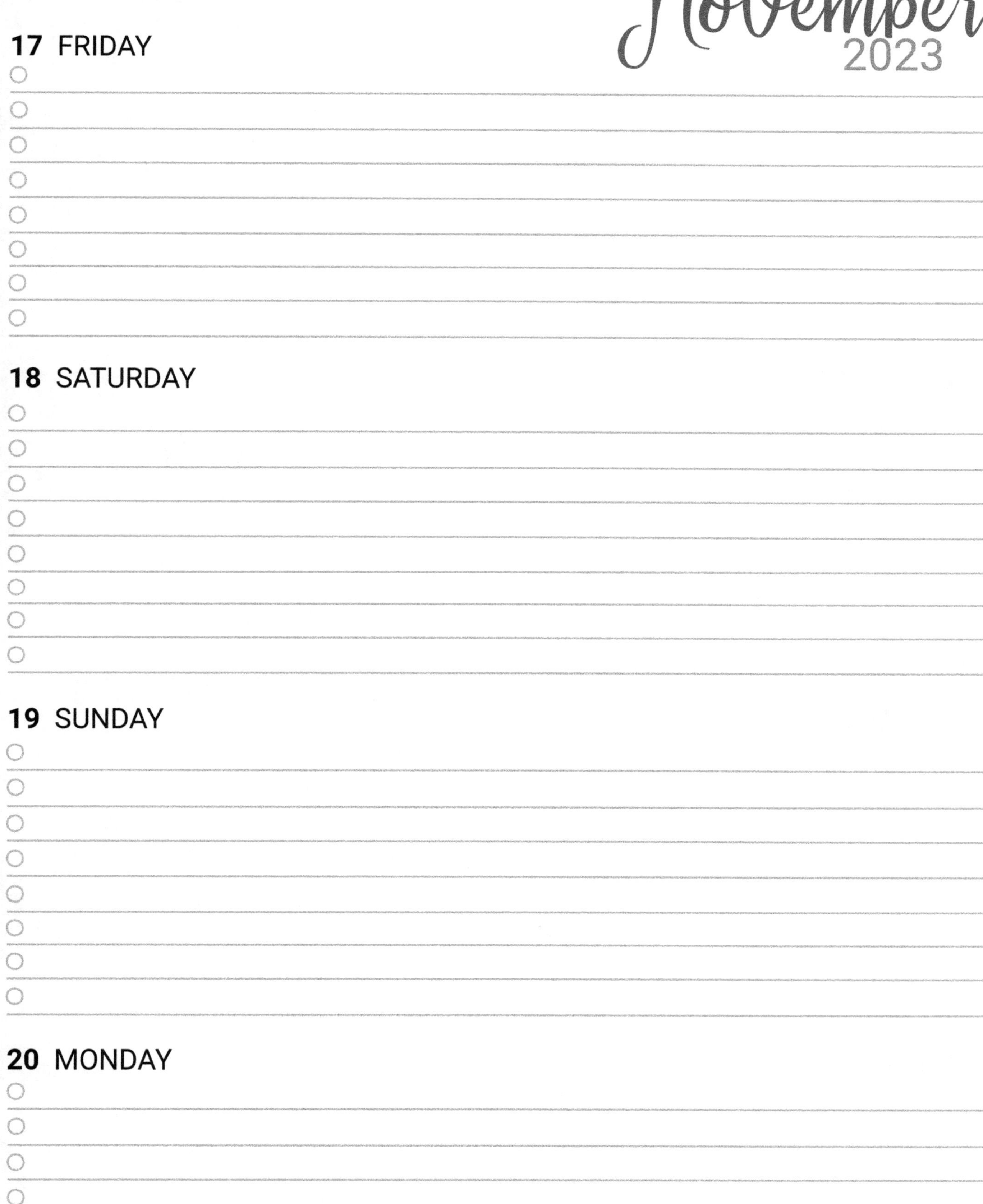

November
2023

17 FRIDAY

18 SATURDAY

19 SUNDAY

20 MONDAY

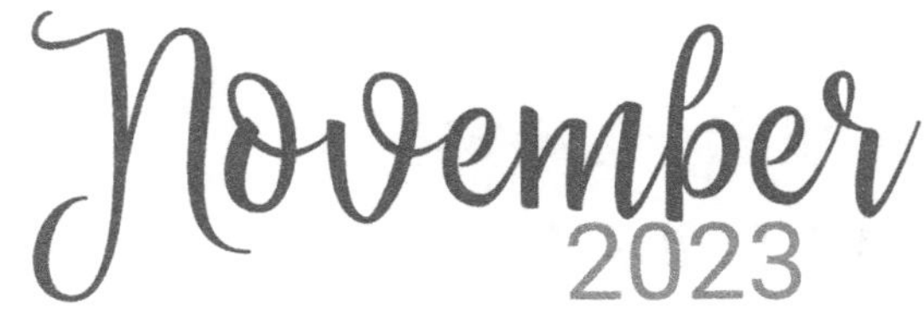

21 TUESDAY

22 WEDNESDAY

23 THURSDAY

24 FRIDAY

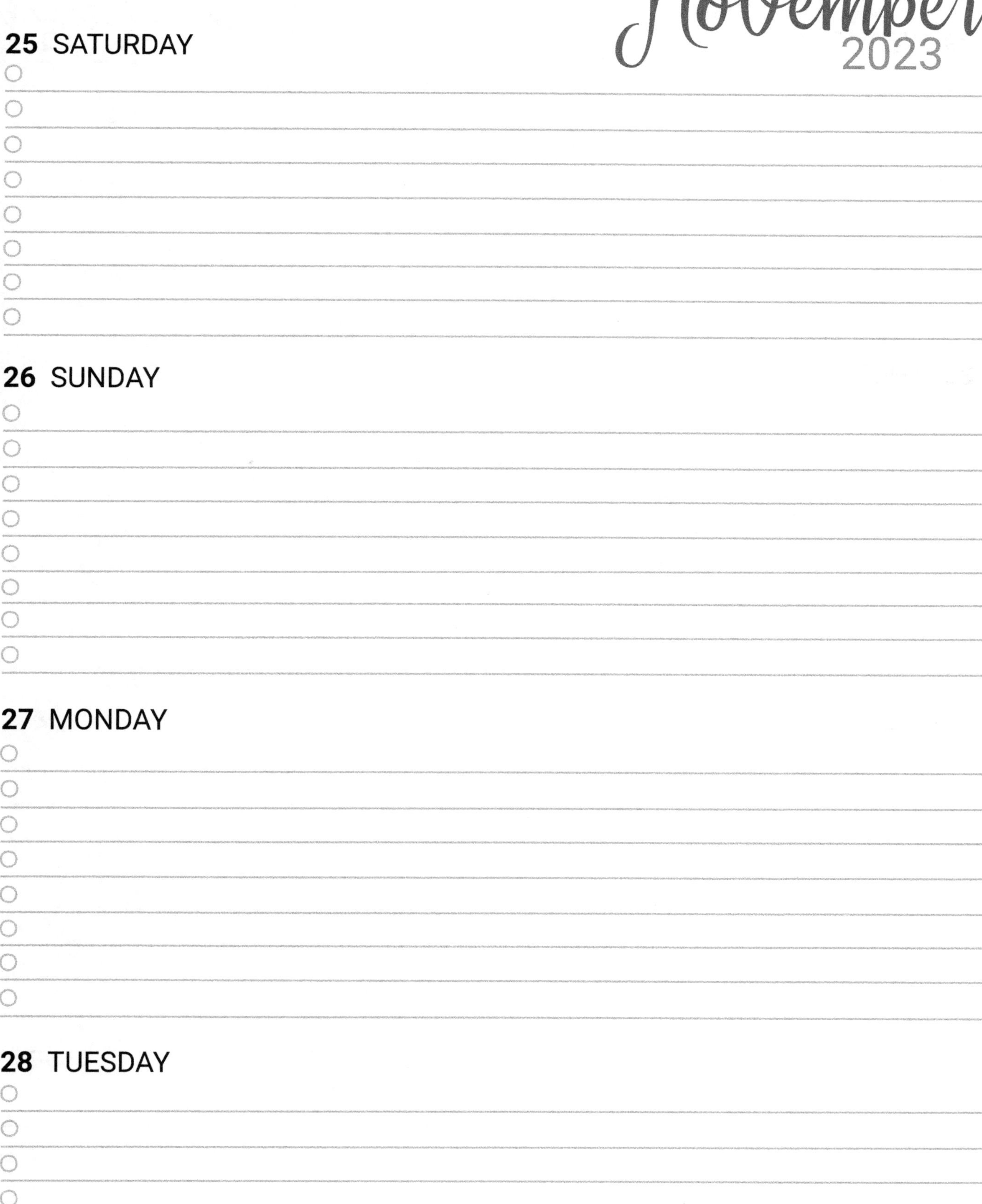

25 SATURDAY

26 SUNDAY

27 MONDAY

28 TUESDAY

29 WEDNESDAY

30 THURSDAY

NOTES

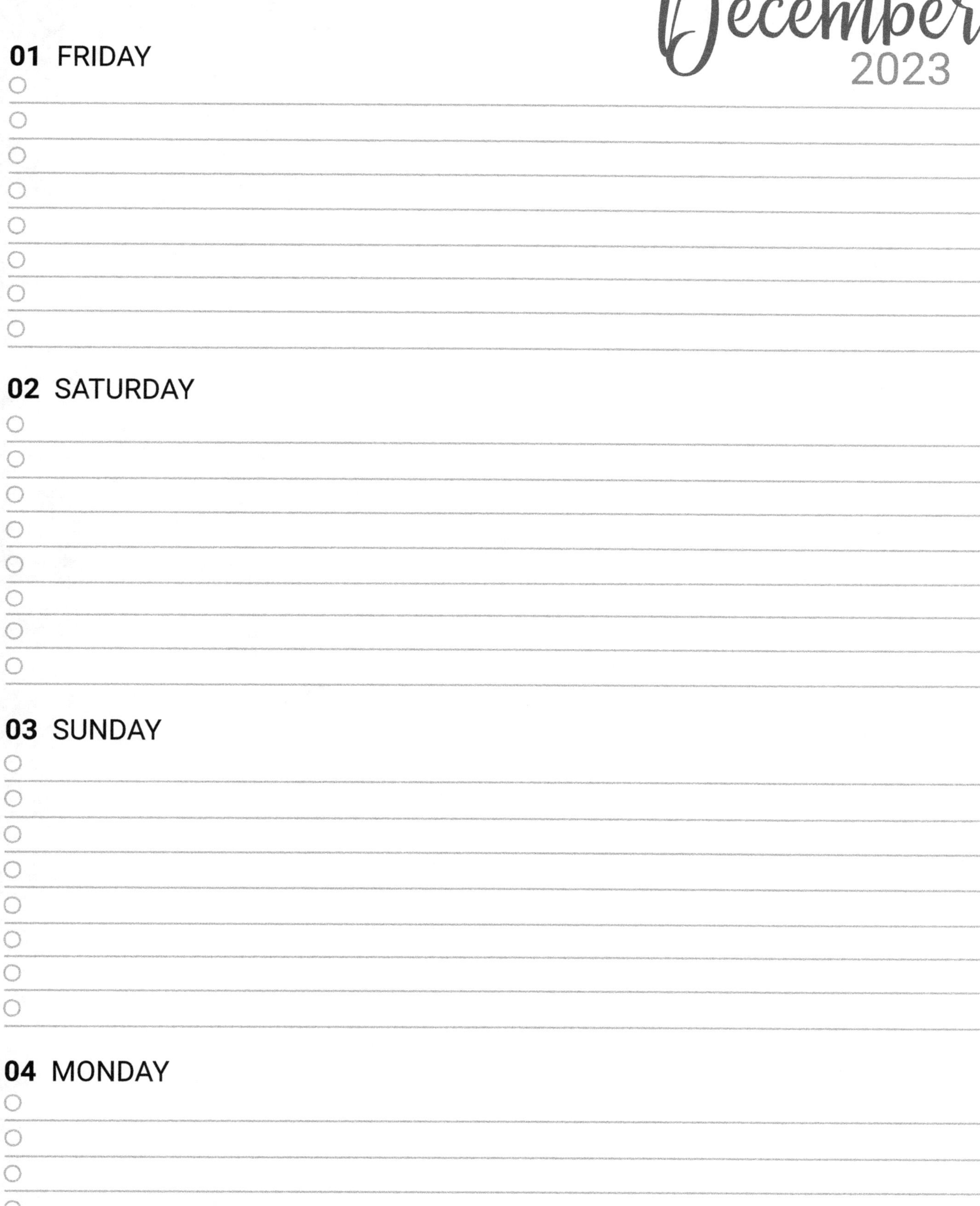

01 FRIDAY

02 SATURDAY

03 SUNDAY

04 MONDAY

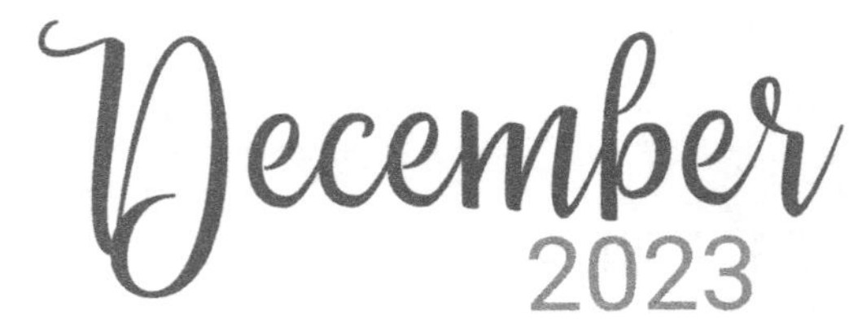

December
2023

05 TUESDAY

06 WEDNESDAY

07 THURSDAY

08 FRIDAY

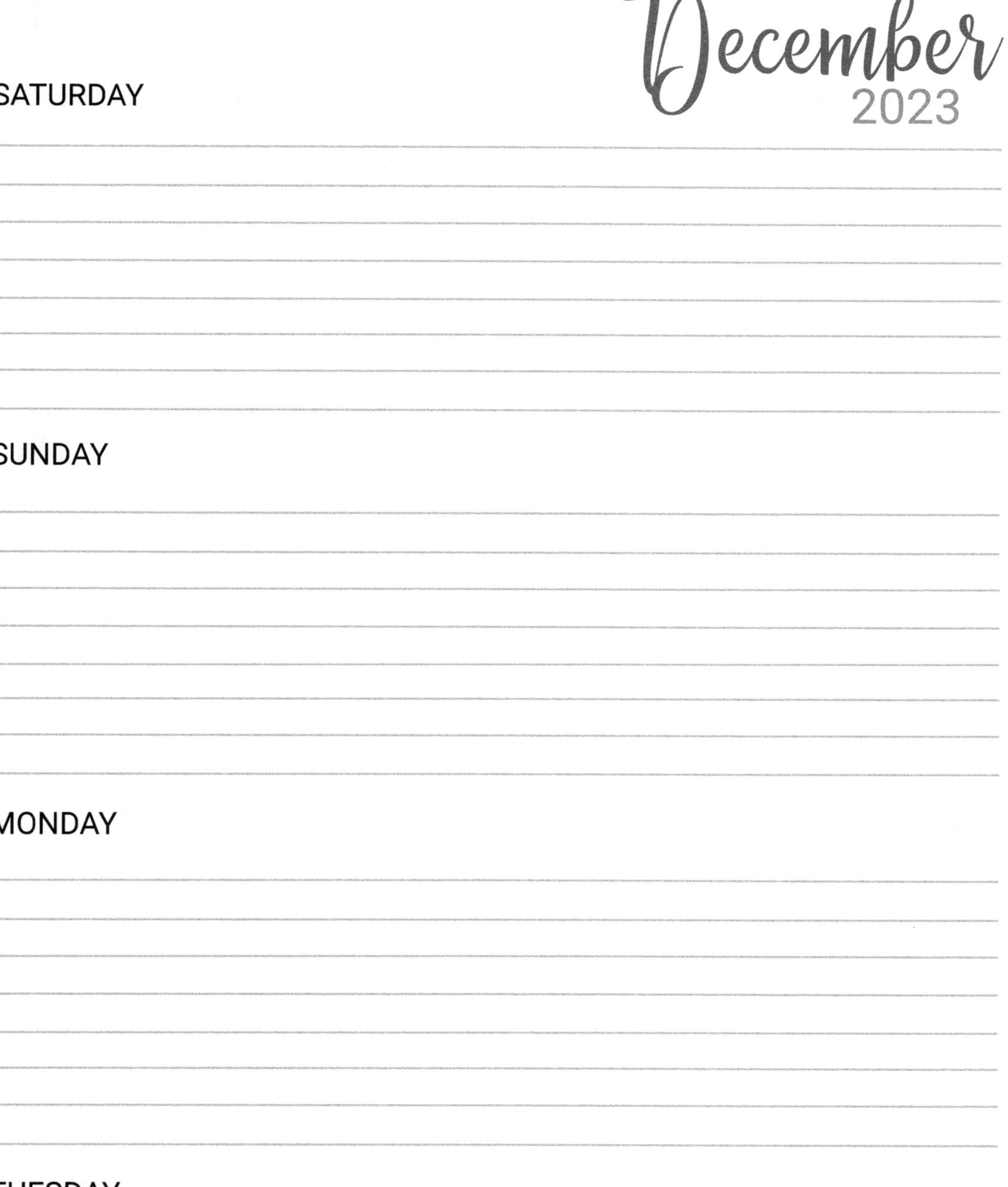

09 SATURDAY

10 SUNDAY

11 MONDAY

12 TUESDAY

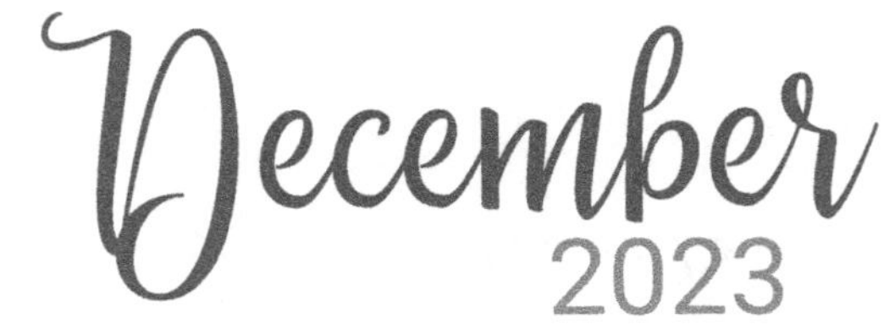

December
2023

13 WEDNESDAY

14 THURSDAY

15 FRIDAY

16 SATURDAY

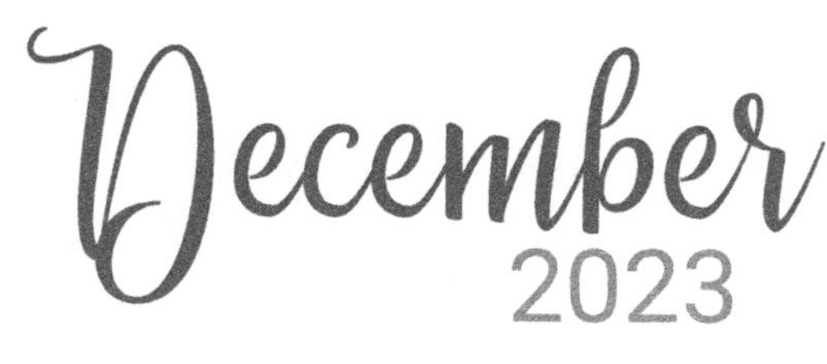

17 SUNDAY

18 MONDAY

19 TUESDAY

20 WEDNESDAY

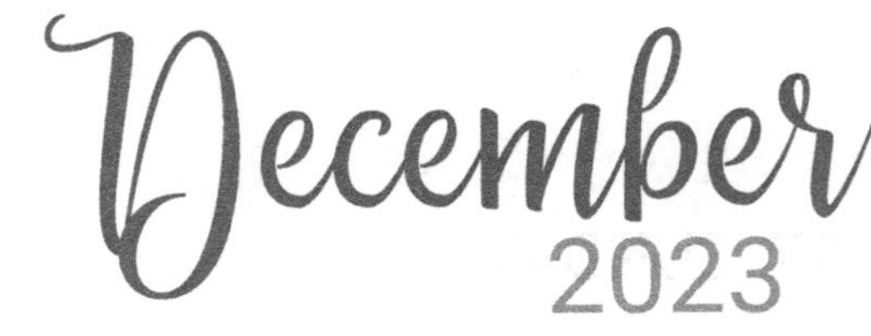

21 THURSDAY

22 FRIDAY

23 SATURDAY

24 SUNDAY

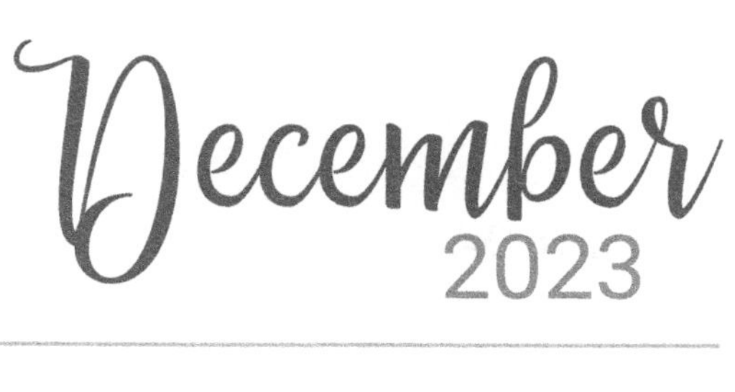

25 MONDAY

26 TUESDAY

27 WEDNESDAY

28 THURSDAY

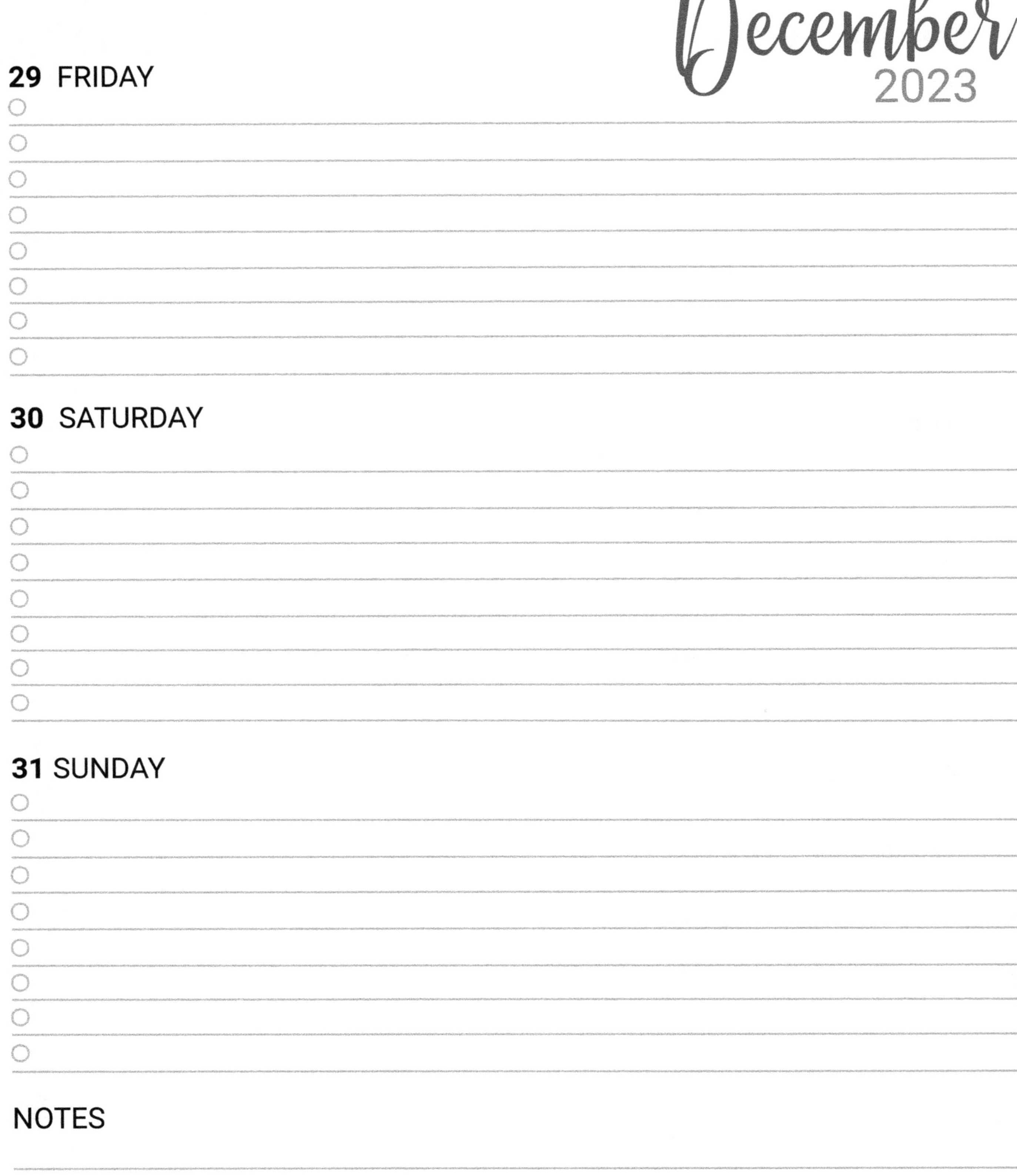

29 FRIDAY

30 SATURDAY

31 SUNDAY

NOTES

www.ingramcontent.com/pod-product-compliance
Lightning Source LLC
Chambersburg PA
CBHW080625041125
34902CB00053B/1534